HOME GROW

H⬥me GROWN Indiana

A Food Lover's Guide to Good Eating in the Hoosier State

CHRISTINE BARBOUR

&

SCOTT HUTCHESON

QUARRY BOOKS

an imprint of

INDIANA UNIVERSITY PRESS

Bloomington & Indianapolis

This book is a publication of

Quarry Books
an imprint of

Indiana University Press
601 North Morton Street
Bloomington, IN 47404-3797 USA

http://iupress.indiana.edu

Telephone orders: 800-842-6796
Fax orders: 812-855-7931
Orders by e-mail: iuporder@indiana.edu

The paper used in this publication meets the minimum requirements of
American National Standard for Information Sciences—Permanence of
Paper for Printed Library Materials, ANSI Z39.48-1984.

Manufactured in the United States of America

www.homegrownindiana.com

Library of Congress Cataloging-in-Publication Data

Barbour, Christine, date–
  Home grown Indiana : a food lover's guide to good eating in the Hoosier
State / Christine Barbour and Scott Hutcheson.
    p. cm.
  Includes indexes.
  ISBN 978-0-253-22019-6 (paper)
  1. Natural foods—Indiana. 2. Cookery (Natural foods) 3. Farm produce—
Indiana—Guidebooks. 4. Natural food restaurants—Indiana—Guide-
books. I. Hutcheson, Scott. II. Title.
  TX369.B363 2008
  641.5'636—dc22
2008009985

1   2   3   4   5   13   12   11   10   09   08

CONTENTS
INDIANA

ACKNOWLEDGMENTS

Writing this book has been filled with delicious surprises, not the least of which is the unexpected treat of our friendship. We are grateful to all the farmers, producers, and chefs who gave us their time and let us into their busy lives to learn more about what they do. We would also like to thank Lori DesRochers, for her research assistance, and all the good people at I.U. Press who made this book happen: Janet Rabinowitch, Anne Clemmer, Jamison Cockerham, Shoshanna Green, and Brian Herrmann.

In addition, Christine thanks her husband Jerry for accompanying her on potato chip and fried chicken adventures and Scott says a big thank you to his wife Lisa and their sons Henry and Oliver. Even though their weekend road trips included a few episodes of getting lost and some wild goose-less chases, spending the time together was loads of fun.

We look forward to hearing from readers about your own great food finds and discoveries here in Indiana. Happy hunting.

Christine Barbour
Scott Hutcheson

HOME GROWN INDIANA

NORTHWEST

NORTHEAST

NORTH CENTRAL

CENTRAL

SOUTHEAST &
SOUTH CENTRAL

SOUTHWEST

SOUTHERN

NORTHWEST

Lake
Porter
La Porte
St. Joseph
Elkhart
Lagrange
Steuben
Newton
Jasper
Starke
Marshall
Kosciusko
Noble
De Kalb
Pulaski
Fulton
Whitley
Allen

NORTHEAST

NORTH CENTRAL

Benton
White
Cass
Miami
Wabash
Huntington
Wells
Adams
Warren
Tippecanoe
Carroll
Howard
Grant
Blackford
Jay
Fountain
Clinton
Tipton
Madison
Delaware
Randolph

CENTRAL

Vermillion
Parke
Montgomery
Boone
Hamilton
Henry
Wayne
Putnam
Hendricks
Marion
Hancock
Rush
Fayette
Union
Vigo
Clay
Owen
Morgan
Johnson
Shelby
Franklin

SOUTHEAST &
SOUTH CENTRAL

Decatur
Bartholomew
Brown
Monroe
Ripley
Dearborn
Sullivan
Greene
Jennings
Ohio
Jefferson
Switzerland

SOUTHWEST

Lawrence
Jackson
Scott
Knox
Daviess
Martin
Washington
Clark
Orange
Pike
Dubois
Crawford
Floyd
Gibson
Posey
Vander-
burgh
Warrick
Spencer
Perry
Harrison

SOUTHERN

INTRODUCTION

This book began the way so many do, with this frustrated response to an unanswered question: "You know, someone should *really* write a book."

We had each posed the question, long before we knew each other. Christine asked it on a gorgeous Indiana day in late July. The Hoosier-blue sky was full of that golden afternoon light that reflects off the corn fields and makes your town-weary heart swell with gladness to be out of the city. "Let's go for a long drive and stop for something to eat along the way," she said to her husband. "The fields are bursting with good fresh food—let's go find some." But where could they go?

A few counties away, Scott was having similar yearnings, obsessed with an Indiana classic. "There are so many pork tenderloin sandwiches on Indiana menus, and so many hogs being raised on Indiana farms. Where can I find a real Hoosier tenderloin made from local pork?" he wondered.

When it came to finding good, local ingredients, neither of us food-savvy Hoosiers really had a clue. We knew that Indiana must have wonderful, unusual places to get home-grown food—farms to visit, markets to explore, restaurants that go the extra mile to source their food locally—but outside of our own backyards, we didn't know where they were. The lovely fields full of corn surrounded towns full of chain restaurants and fast-food places. Every charming country lane seemed to lead, eventually, to a burger and fries. Somewhere there had to be local gems, but they remained hidden from the casual traveler. Where were they? Someone, we thought, should really write a book.

Four years later, here we are.

Christine is a political science professor at Indiana University, teaching about the politics of food and writing about food for local publications. Also the co-director of Slow Food Bloomington, she has long been interested in local food and farmers, and a few years ago she began keeping notes about places she'd visited and written about. Scott works in economic development for Purdue University and spends a lot of time on the road in Indiana. He chronicles his travels and his discoveries of local food on a blog he calls *The Hungry Hoosier,* and he also writes about food for local publications.

The two of us, traveling parallel paths in parallel universes (though at rival universities), might never have met without the Internet. They say you should beware of people you meet in cyberspace, but in this case the result of the email correspondence we struck up when Christine began to read Scott's blog was pure serendipity. Both of us wanted to compile information on local food, and neither had time to cover the whole state. So we divvied up the work and travel, and soon it became clear that the "someone" who should write a book was us.

Home Grown Indiana is the result.

Why Eat Local?

In a day when most food travels an average of 1,300 miles from field to dinner plate and some produce comes to Indiana from as far away as China, there is something reassuring about knowing that we can supply almost all our nutritional needs with food that is grown or raised right here in our state.

First, for the obvious reason: local food is almost always fresher and more delicious than food that has been bred to spend long hours traveling across the world to reach our kitchens. Just-picked asparagus tastes like nothing else in the world—grassy and earthy and fragrant with spring. Corn from the garden is toothsome and milky and almost candy-sweet. Tender greens for the salad, spicy tomatoes, and crisp cucumbers bear no resemblance to their supermarket shadows. All local food does not taste better than all imported food, of course, but when scientists breed food to withstand long-haul transportation, flavor is often among the first things to go.

Local food, too, is likely to include the idiosyncratic and quirky items that for one reason or another can't make it on the mass market. The nearly forgotten varieties of fruits, vegetables, meats, and poultry that our grandparents took for granted have become rare delicacies in an age where tomatoes are bred for year-round availability and picture-perfect appearance, turkeys for large quantities of white meat, and pigs for an unpiglike leanness. Heirloom tomatoes, cat-faced and split, may have no shelf life, but that's okay when you can't resist eating them warm from the sun. Heritage turkeys may need to be brined before roasting, but their flavor is rich and true and much closer to something the Pilgrims would recognize than that of a Butterball bird could ever be. And pastured pork may lose its advertising value as "the other white meat," but its juicy, porky goodness makes up in flavor what it loses in marketability.

Local food is also, by and large, better for us. At least it gives us the chance to ask: How was this food raised? Since there is a good chance that at least some of whatever chemicals, drugs, hormones, or toxins were used to raise our food will find their way into our bodies when we eat it, surely we have the right to know what we are risking. Were chemicals and pesticides used in this garden? How has that corn been genetically modified? Were those apples sprayed? What was this cow fed? Was it sick when it was slaughtered? What was added to that chicken's feed? What's in this milk, anyway? Hormones, antibiotics? How can we know? Buying local gives us the opportunity to ask the farmer who raised the food what went into it, or at least to ask someone who knows the farmer, and with that knowledge we can make informed decisions about what we eat.

Chances are, local food will have been raised more humanely, too. Vegetables are not sentient beings, but cows and pigs and chickens are. Did they have a good life, before dying to sustain ours? If that's a question that matters to you, buying local offers a way to find out. Even feeding cows on grain and keeping chickens confined can be done in respectful and humane ways when it is done on a small, manageable scale. Ask.

And then there is sustainability. Not only does buying local give us information about the additives that go into raising our food, but it also means that the carbon footprint of our food is smaller because it hasn't traveled the world to get to us. In fact, you may decide that eating locally grown foods raised non-organically is better for the environment than importing organic vegetables from Brazil. Again, when we buy local, we can ask: Was this food grown sustainably? Is the farm that raised it certified organic? If not, why not? Many small farmers refuse to pay a fee to the government for the privilege of organic certification, or flat-out can't afford to do so, but their crops are grown even more naturally than the law requires. Let them tell you how they do it.

Buying local can help keep local economies vital and thriving. Every time you spend a dollar, you put money in someone's pocket. Why not let that pocket be a neighbor's? Supporting local farms and businesses helps preserve our options, too. A chain grocery or restaurant has to be able to market across communities, and often that makes it less able to respond to local needs and preferences.

And of course there is the often overlooked fact that eating local food is just plain more fun. Shopping at the farmers' market can be a joyous experience, filled with chances to meet old friends and make new ones. Picking your own berries is a great day in the sun, as is stopping at a pumpkin festival to choose the Halloween jack-o-lantern and maybe get a hayride in the bargain. Teaching kids about where their food comes from, visiting a farm to pet the goats, moo at the cows, and feed the chickens, is not only a great way to spend family time but also gives a new generation the chance to experience the farm life that their grandparents knew so well and to have a healthy respect for what goes into the work of keeping their tummies full.

The Local Bandwagon

There are many groups preaching the "Eat Local" gospel these days. Chief among them is Slow Food (www .slowfoodusa.org), an international movement dedicated to supporting local farmers, preserving traditional and artisanal methods of food production, and celebrating the pleasures of the table. Slow Food has local chapters (called convivia) all over the world, and four of them in Indiana (Indy, Bloomington, Kentuckiana, and Michiana). More are in the works. As well, local growers' organizations around the state promote their members' products and educate the public about the joys of eating locally and strengthening the link between farm and table. And then there is the Indiana Foodways Alliance (indianafoodways.com), a statewide non-profit organization "dedicated to the celebration, promotion and preservation of the authentic food culture of Indiana," and the Greater Midwest Foodways Alliance (www .greatermidwestfoodways.com), which has a similar mission but covers a larger terrain.

We belong to or work with many of these groups. This book aims to complement their work with practical information about where to go to buy and eat local food. Its audience is the family out for a drive on a sunny summer afternoon, looking for lunch and a fun day out; the cook who wants to stock his or her home kitchen with the finest and freshest ingredients; and the professional chef who, out of personal commitment or a determination to respond to customer demands, decides to source more food locally.

About the Book

We have divided the state, somewhat arbitrarily, into seven regions. Scott took the three regions in the northern half of the state, Christine took the three in the south, and we split the middle. For each region we provide from five to more than a dozen long profiles of significant local food producers or actors in that area—people, organizations, or businesses whose story we wanted to tell at greater length. We follow them with shorter descriptions of other producers, and all the information you need to contact them, plan a visit, or buy their food.

We also catalogue restaurants in each region that make an effort to source their food locally, providing names, addresses, and contact information. The restaurants vary in their commitment to the local cause—they may simply be content to use a local salad mix or a few ripe tomatoes in season, or they may make a more substantial effort, shopping at the farmers' markets themselves and working with farmers to get exactly the food they want. We have profiled many of the chefs who make local foods the centerpiece of their work, and in some cases have coaxed recipes out of them for the home cook to try. There are 18 such recipes in the book and more on our website, www.homegrownindiana.com. As more restaurants make the leap to sourcing food locally, we will use the website to keep you updated.

Finally, each chapter has a list of wineries, breweries and brewpubs, and food festivals in the region—places and events that can be worked into any local foods itinerary. Not all of them use local ingredients (not all wineries get their grapes from Indiana, for instance, and breweries generally do not grow hops and barley themselves), but they are creating an artisanal product that is distinctly Indiana all the same.

Altogether, we locate more than 400 delicious destinations on Indiana's culinary map, including more than 160 profiles and detailed information on 240 additional farms, artisans, restaurants, shops, food festivals, farmers' markets, retailers, wineries, microbreweries, and other people and places—all representing the best of home-grown Indiana foods.

Though wide-ranging, this compilation is not complete, as the local food scene is changing all the time. This book is intended to get you started building a local food network of your own. If we can point you to a chicken guy in your area, chances are he can give you a lead on who's growing heirloom tomatoes or whatever else you are searching for. *Home Grown Indiana* is a work in progress, and future editions will include new places that spring up and remove old ones that fold. We welcome your feedback and suggestions for those revisions.

Keep this book with you—in the glove compartment of your car or in your backpack. Fold down the pages of your favorite producers, make notes of new discoveries, and when you do bring it in the house, don't worry about getting splatters and spills on the pages as you try out the recipes. This is a book that is meant to be useful, so let it develop the dog-eared look of an old friend.

We hope this book will be your guide to good eating in the Hoosier state. Despite the best of intentions, you won't always eat local; believe us, we know. We'd like to say you'll never see us buying grocery-store lettuce in a bag or grabbing a fast-food sandwich, but chances are you will. With the best will in the world to slow things down, our lives still get hectic, and we can't make every meal a leisurely local feast. But the decision about what to eat is a thousand small choices every day, and we can get some of them, many of them, right, even if others fall through the cracks. Every choice we make, every dollar we spend on food, is a vote for the way we want to live our lives.

Local, slow, quirky, and delicious versus imported, fast, standardized, and tasteless. For us, it's no choice at all. Happy travels and good eating!

Please contact us! We can be reached through our website, www.homegrownindiana.com, and through our individual blogs, Christine's *My Plate or Yours?* (www .myplateoryours.net) and Scott's *The Hungry Hoosier* (www.hungryhoosier.com).

1

Northwest

Northwest Indiana has always suffered a bit from an identity crisis. Is it suburban Chicago or Hoosier territory? The answer, of course, is "Both!"

The impact of the Second City here is undeniable. In the early 1900s, the South Shore Line provided easy transportation between Chicago and South Bend, as well as to several places in between. It allowed greater numbers of Hoosiers to commute to Chicago to work and also brought Chicagoans across the border to play. Urbanization created the critical mass for an interesting local food culture.

Although the South Shore Line is still popular, most people now traverse the region by interstate and toll road. Get just a few miles out from the transportation arteries and northwest Indiana is unmistakably rural. This urban/rural mix is the perfect recipe for a growing local foods movement that ranges from freshwater caviar and a world-class spice house to organic heirloom tomatoes and award-winning cheese. "Da Region" boasts some terrific restaurants, loads of family farms, and a growing network of people trying to weave it all together into the a true local foods movement (see www.southshorelocalfoods.org).

Collins Caviar

CAVIAR

113 York St., Michigan City IN 46360 (LaPorte)
219-809-8100 • www.collinscaviar.com

When it comes to Indiana's claim-to-fame foods, breaded tenderloin sandwiches and sugar cream pies come to mind. But Hoosiers can also count as their own a few national brand names, like Red Gold tomatoes and Clabber Girl baking soda. Even Wonder Bread and Papa John's have Hoosier roots.

Here's another one to add to the list. In 2005, Indiana became home to one of the nation's finest domestic freshwater caviar houses. Collins Caviar was founded in Chicago in 1983, when mother and daughter Carolyn and Rachel Collins decided to start making caviar. Carolyn and Rachel were avid anglers, and after seeing the beautiful roe of the Lake Michigan Chinook salmon they caught, they set out to learn how to transform the raw roe into succulent caviar.

This was no easy task. The roe-to-caviar transformation requires the science of Galileo and the artistry of Monet. Carolyn and Rachel eventually cracked the code, and their caviar became a hit with family and friends. When they first served it to a chef friend he insisted on having some for his restaurant, and a business was born. It was not long before they moved out of the home kitchen into a production facility in Chicago.

After just a few years they had reached legend-like status among caviar enthusiasts and had been heralded in the "foodie" media, including the *New York Times* and *Bon Appetit*. Along the way Carolyn retired, leaving the business completely in Rachel's capable hands. A couple of years ago, a series of circumstances led Rachel to look for a new location in northwest Indiana, and Michigan City took the prize.

We recently had an opportunity to spend most of the day with Rachel Collins, getting quite an education about caviar and her company. We also got to sample several of her products, and we must say, they were magnificent. Prior to our visit, our caviar consumption had been somewhat limited—the occasional caviar-garnished maki roll, or the holiday buffet table. After the day with Collins, we were hooked. Like great seafood, first-rate caviar is not fishy but tastes like the best of what the ocean has to offer—fresh, clean, and salty.

Collins Caviar offers a varied line of products, including caviar from freshwater salmon, whitefish, hackleback, and paddlefish. Collins also has some great infused products—caviars flavored with Citron vodka, wasabi, and other great flavors. It also offers several caviar crème spreads that are out of this world. Some of these come in a pastry bag, complete with plastic tip, ready to be squeezed out into designs as pleasing to the eye as to the mouth. These flavor-infused caviars are amazing, and the crème spreads are rich and decadent. Consult the website for scheduled events, including hosted tastings throughout the year. Visits can also be arranged.

County Line Orchard

APPLES, CIDER, BAKED GOODS

200 County Line Rd., Hobart IN 46342 (Lake)
219-947-4477 • www.countylineorchard.com

County Line Orchard began operation in 1987, when Dave McAfee planted his first tree, but the family's farming tradition in Hobart goes back five generations.

McAfee worked the family farm as a boy but went on to other pursuits for a while before he returned to Hobart to transform the family farm from traditional crop production to an apple orchard.

County Line Orchard currently grows about 20 different varieties of apples, which are listed on its website along with helpful information about which are best suited for eating fresh, making pies, etc. Much thought went into selecting these 20 varieties, with taste as the primary concern. County Line is committed to growing the best-tasting apples even if that means some of the varieties are not the most beautiful. Another priority was to have ripe apples available for as long as possible. The first apples are ready in early August and the last in early November.

County Line offers both U-Pick apples and, in the onsite store, those they have picked for you. The store also sells treats like freshly dipped caramel apples, beguiling apple-cinnamon donuts, and fresh-baked bread. A Sweet Shop offers ice cream, fudge, and other temptations. On weekends, lunch and dinner is served at the County Line Grill—brats and angus burgers, chicken breasts, and veggie burgers, and fresh corn on the cob when it is in season.

Honey is also available in the store, and the Observation Hives, nearby in the Bee Barn, are a popular attraction. The Bee Barn is just one of several buildings at County Line Orchard, most of which were moved to the location from other nearby farms and lovingly restored. One of the most recent arrivals is the Barn at County Line Orchard, which can be rented for wedding receptions and other special events and can accommodate up to 300 guests. The historic structure has been renovated to include modern conveniences, including a 2,550-square-foot hardwood dance floor.

There are lots of activities for kids at County Line—a chick hatchery, a petting zoo, and a kid-size bovine-painted train called the MooChoo. Weekend attractions during apple season include face painting, scarecrow making, and puppet shows that will keep little ones entertained. County Line is a popular destination during the Halloween season for its Trail of Fears, Haunted Barn, and Corn Maize.

County Line has an extensive website with a great deal of information about its operation. Offerings vary throughout the year, so if you are planning a visit, check the website for opening hours and special events. During the school year, there can be as many as 1,000 children there at any given time, and nearly 40,000 students and teachers visit over the course of the year on field trips. If that is not your cup of tea, visit after 2:30 PM on a weekday. Family passes are available.

Fair Oaks Farms

DAIRY

> 856 N. 600 E., Fair Oaks IN 47943 (Newton)
> 877-536-1194 • www.fofarms.com

If you've traveled I-65 between Lafayette and Chicago, you have no doubt seen the billboards for Fair Oaks Farms in Newton County. It is a family farm grown to the scale of a large enterprise, one of the largest dairies in the U.S. Fair Oaks is a fully integrated operation, which means this one business does it all: grows the feed, raises the cows, does the milking, processes the milk, makes the ice cream and cheese, and sells its products. The staff have it down to a science, but judging by the accolades for their products, they've not lost sight of the art.

Fair Oaks is sort of a high-lactose version of Disneyworld for the whole family, with interactive exhibits, guided tours, and lots of really good food. Visitors get to witness nearly every part of the From Grass-to-Glass™ operation. Since about 80 calves are born on the farm each day, nearly every tour gets to witness a birth. Tours can also include a "4-D" movie and animatronic cows and trees.

When you visit Fair Oaks, be sure to arrive hungry. Not only can you watch cheese being made, you can also enjoy a wide variety of food and buy some to take home. The café serves breakfast and lunch as well as lots of snacks. Nearly every item, of course, features Fair Oaks' products. You can choose a breakfast burrito in the morning or opt for a grilled cheese sandwich or a quesadilla for lunch. Wash it all down with a latte and satisfy your sweet tooth with some boutique ice cream.

For serious food lovers, the main attraction of the cheese factory is the cheese counter. The knowledgeable staff can walk you through the many choices—Asiago, Cheddar, Gouda, Havarti, mozzarella, Muenster, Swiss, and more—and provide samples as they go. A favorite is their award-winning Emmentaler. This slightly sweet and nutty cheese is rich and creamy. It melts terrifically for fondue and pairs nicely with fruit and a not-too-dry white wine. This cheese was selected as the Overall Winner in the 2005 U.S. Championship Cheese Contest. Another of our favorites is the Sweet Swiss, which won a Best of Class award in 2005. Smooth and buttery with, as the name suggests, a hint of sweetness, it is an original creation of Fair Oaks master cheese maker Randy Krahenbuhl.

Fair Oaks cheeses are showing up in increasing numbers on the menus of Indiana chefs. Fair Oaks maintains an impressive online store, so restaurants and home cooks alike can get award-winning cheeses delivered right to their doors. Whether you visit in person or shop online, Fair Oaks should not be missed. It is open seven days a week from 8:30 AM to 6:00 PM.

Hiatt's Pork and Poultry

CHICKEN, TURKEY, DUCK, GOOSE, RABBIT

> Booth at the South Bend Farmers' Market
> 1105 Northside Blvd., South Bend IN 46615 (St. Joseph)
> 574-282-1259

The Hiatt family has been a fixture at the South Bend Farmers' Market since 1917, when Chauncey Hiatt began selling poultry there. As corner grocery stores and mega-supermarkets opened their doors, folks in South Bend continued to patronize Hiatt's. Chauncey eventually turned the reins over to his son Clarence, and Hiatt's is now in the capable hands of the third and fourth generations. Gene Hiatt and his son Michael, along with lots of love and support from Gene's wife Ruth, carry on the nearly 100-year-old business. Gene's five small grandchildren are now in the picture, so another 100 years looks promising.

On their Rochester farm, the Hiatts raise chickens, turkeys, ducks, and geese. All the birds are raised without drugs, and they have plenty of room to run loose and do whatever it is that chickens, turkeys, ducks, and geese like to do. Neighbor kids raise rabbits, which the Hiatts process and sell at the market as well. Although they don't raise their own hogs, the Hiatts sell pork products, including various cuts and a variety of sausages, that they have bought from others.

The Hiatts process all their birds themselves every week and sell only fresh poultry, not frozen. Chickens are by far the most popular product and they are sold as whole birds, in halves, in quarters, and in individual parts, including boneless skinless breasts. Bags of chicken feet are also popular, being used to make rich and flavorful stock.

Broad-breasted turkeys are sold year-round, but Thanksgiving, of course, is when demand is highest. Thanksgiving birds can be preordered beginning in October. The Hiatts sell more than 1,000 turkeys each year. They also offer ground turkey. Ducks and geese are also sold year-round, but their sales peak at Christmas and New Year.

With four generations of experience eating their own birds, the Hiatts have developed some tried-and-true cooking techniques which they gladly share with customers. When it comes to roasting a turkey, they recommend starting out at a very high heat—450 degrees or so—for about 20 minutes, to crisp the skin and seal in the juices. The oven temperature can then be reduced to about 325 degrees until the bird is done. This will result in a juicy and flavor-packed bird. Ducks and geese are terrific stuffed with sauerkraut and roasted, a tip from the Hiatts' German heritage. Ducks and geese are fatty birds, and the sauerkraut absorbs much of the fat and also imparts a terrific flavor. After the bird is cooked, the sauerkraut is a delicious side dish.

The Hiatts' poultry is only available at the South Bend Farmers' Market. Their booth is open year-round on Tuesdays and Thursdays from 7:00 AM to 2:00 PM and Saturdays from 7:00 AM to 3:00 PM, and from May through September it is also open on Fridays from 7:00 AM to 2:00 PM. Farm visits are not available.

Kelly's Table at Creekwood Inn

RESTAURANT

5727 N. 600 W., Michigan City IN 46360 (LaPorte)
219-872-5624 • www.kellyscreekwood.com

When Patricia Kelly Molden was growing up, the center of her family's home was always the dining room, where everyone gathered nightly to share food, news, and stories about their day. Dinner parties were common in the Kelly household, and Pat and her nine siblings served as waitresses, bus staff, cooks, and dishwashers—great training for her future vocation.

Her journey since then has included stops with the late chef John Snowden of Dumas Père École de la Cuisine Française and as a pastry chef, and later head chef, in Rochester, New York. She eventually settled in northwest Indiana and continued her culinary career by catering and writing cookbooks. Several years ago she seized the opportunity to open her own restaurant. "Kelly's Table was created in a spirit of fond remembrance for those exciting parties where my love of food, entertaining, and sharing good times was born," Pat Molden explains.

Kelly's Table adjoins the Creekwood Inn, a bed and breakfast nestled amidst 30 acres of walnut, oak, and pine trees, near a fork in Willow Creek. The menu is an eclectic mix of some reinterpretations of Kelly family favorites and creations Molden has developed over the years. The menu is seasonal, changing regularly to take advantage of choice ingredients from both near and far. Quality ingredients and skilled execution are apparent in even the simplest dishes at Kelly's Table.

After fixing breakfast for the overnight guests at the Inn, Molden dashes over to the farmers' market to see what she can get for the day ahead. Some of her mainstays are smoky bacon, eggs, chicken, duck, and an assortment of poultry livers for her famous paté. During the growing season, she grabs as much fresh produce and as many herbs as possible. When she returns to her kitchen all these raw ingredients get transformed into homemade stocks, soups, and all manner of entrées, side dishes, and desserts. When she scrambles farm-fresh eggs for the Inn's guests at breakfast, she is always asked for the "secret ingredient" that makes them such a rich yellow and so flavor-packed. Kelly's Table is open Wednesdays though Saturdays from 5:00 to 9:00 PM and reservations are recommended.

WINE-BRAISED BISON BRISKET

Pat Molden, the chef and proprietor at Kelly's Table at Creekwood Inn in LaPorte, gets rave reviews for this bison brisket. She uses bison from nearby Prairie Hills Bison Farm. This brisket cooks at a very low temperature so the extra-lean meat does not dry out.

- 1 locally raised bison brisket, about 5 pounds
- 1 tablespoon whole-grain mustard
- 1 tablespoon chopped garlic
- Coarsely ground black pepper
- 2 medium carrots, sliced
- 1 onion, sliced
- 1 stalk celery, chopped
- 2 bay leaves
- 1 teaspoon thyme leaves
- 1 bottle (750 ml) red wine, preferably Merlot or Zinfandel
- 2 tablespoons olive oil

· 3 cups beef broth or bison broth (use homemade if possible; otherwise be sure to use a reduced-sodium variety)
· Salt and pepper, to taste
· Farm-market fingerling potatoes, cooked, warm

Place brisket in large non-metallic container or plastic bag. Combine mustard, garlic, and pepper and rub over brisket. Place vegetables and herbs on top of brisket, and pour wine over it. Marinate, refrigerated, 12 days.

Remove brisket from marinade, reserving marinade. Dry meat with paper towels. Heat oil in large skillet; sear meat until well browned on both sides. Place in braising pan or Dutch oven. Pour marinade and broth over meat; cover pan. Heat to simmering on top of stove. Place pan in 200° oven. Cook until tender, about 3 hours. Do not let the liquid boil, and be careful not to overcook the meat. Bison is very lean, and needs careful cooking so it does not dry out.

Remove meat from pan and keep warm. Strain braising liquid, discarding vegetables, and remove fat. Boil liquid until thick and syrupy, about 20 minutes. Season to taste with salt and pepper. Slice meat carefully across the grain. Serve with potatoes, carrots, and sauce. Serves 6–8.

Marilyn's Bakery and Dinner on the Terrace

PRODUCE, BAKED GOODS, RESTAURANT

8960 E. Ridge Rd., Hobart IN 46342 (Lake)
219-962-BAKE (2253) • www.marilynsbakery.com

Much of the fun of dinner parties comes from the mix of people brought together for the occasion. That is also part of the enjoyment of a Dinner on the Terrace at Marilyn's

Bakery, part of Johnson's Market in Hobart. Did you get all that? This is what you call a "three-fer"—produce market, bakery, and restaurant.

The bakery is currently in the capable hands of Barb Tracy, Marilyn's daughter. It was founded as a way to add some value to the fruits they grew to supply Johnson's Market. Its early claim to fame was pies—apple, cherry, blueberry, and the like. Pies are still a big part of the business, but the pastry repertoire has expanded to include everything that you expect in a top-notch bakery. Fruits for the pies come from the market and other nearby suppliers. In the off-season, Tracy uses fruit that was frozen earlier in the year.

The Dinner on the Terrace is served only about five times a year, between mid-July and the first of October. Tracy began offering dinner primarily to have a chance to paint occasionally with a broader culinary brush and to share with others her philosophy on food and eating. Tracy also admits that between running the bakery business and raising a child, she and her husband have no time for a social life. The dinners give them an opportunity to meet new people. They are communal, jovial events, each bringing together an eclectic group of 20–24 diners who make the conversation almost as interesting as the food. When we visited, our table included a dealer in antique violins, an art gallery owner, a chef from another restaurant, Rachel Collins of Collins Caviar (p. 12), the owner of a PR agency, and the owner of the reverie spa (p. 33). See what we mean?

The dinners are gourmet vegetarian affairs, each offering five full courses. Each is based on the foods that are in season at that time, many of which are grown by Tracy's family. The events are promoted primarily by word of mouth, but tentative menus can be found on the website. The meal is served, as you might guess, outside on the terrace. Lucky diners will get to hear a summer rain shower echo off the terrace's tin roof. The evening typically begins with Tracy explaining her philosophy of food and eating—local, seasonal, letting the fruits and vegetables stand on their own with minimal interference from the chef. When we were there, Tracy's seasonal menu included such stand-out courses as French-Fried Eggplant with a Savory Cheese-Filled Pear, Beet Soup, and Caramelized Shallot Quinoa with Butternut Squash. Each course was simple, straightforward, and delicious, fully embodying Tracy's philosophy. No alcohol is served, but diners are encouraged to bring their own wines. Tracy will often join diners for the entrée, and both the wine and the conversation can flow for hours. These dinners fill up quickly, so plan ahead and call for reservations.

QUINOA WITH FALL BUTTERNUT SQUASH AND PEANUT TOFU SAUCE

This is one of Barbara Tracy's favorite fall dishes. It is frequently part of her seasonal Dinners on the Terrace at Marilyn's Bakery. Although it is a vegetarian entrée, she has pleased even her most carnivorous friends with it. Quinoa is a high-protein South American grain. When roasted, it has a wonderful nutty aroma. Pick up a butternut squash at the local farmers' market.

Marinated Tofu
- 4 tablespoons soy sauce
- 4 tablespoons cooking sherry
- 2 cloves garlic, minced
- 1 tablespoon rice wine vinegar
- 1 package extra-firm tofu, cubed

Quinoa and Squash

- 2½ cups quinoa
- ¼ stick butter (or 2 tablespoons of any oil)
- 2 tablespoons olive oil
- 1 onion, diced
- 4 stalks celery, diced
- 1 butternut squash, peeled, seeded, and chopped into bite-size pieces
- 3 cups vegetable stock
- 2 bay leaves

Peanut Sauce

- ½ cup water
- 1 tablespoon minced garlic
- 2 tablespoons soy sauce
- 2 heaping tablespoons natural peanut butter
- 1 tablespoon coconut milk

In a medium bowl, whisk together soy sauce, sherry, garlic, and vinegar. Add tofu, cover with plastic, and marinate in the refrigerator for at least 2 hours, overnight if possible.

Preheat oven to 325°. Rinse the quinoa until the water runs clean. Spread quinoa out on a baking sheet and roast at 325° until dry and toasted, stirring occasionally. Remove baking sheet from the oven but leave the oven on. Heat butter or oil in a stock pot over medium heat and sauté onion and celery until soft. Add roasted quinoa and squash and stir until well coated. Add stock and bay leaves. Raise heat to high and bring to a boil, then reduce heat and simmer for about 25 minutes until all liquid is absorbed.

While stock is simmering, place the tofu pieces on the cooking sheet and bake for 10–12 minutes. Remove from the oven to turn over the pieces, return to the oven to bake for 10 minutes more.

To make the sauce, bring the water to a boil in a saucepan. Turn off the heat, add soy sauce, garlic, peanut butter, and coconut milk, and mix thoroughly. To serve, plate the quinoa and squash, top with tofu, and pour sauce over. Serves about 6.

Al's Supermarkets

PRODUCE

Many northwest Indiana locations (LaPorte and Porter)
219-879-3357 • www.alssupermarkets.com

Al's Supermarkets began in 1946 as a corner fruit and vegetable stand. Three generations later, the family business has grown to include five Al's Supermarkets in Indiana and Barney's Market in nearby New Buffalo, Michigan. From the beginning, Al's has worked with local growers, from a hobby gardener with a single bushel of green beans to a farmer with fields of sweet corn, to provide customers with more local produce. When you shop at Al's, the helpful staff can help point out which products are local. For locations and hours of operations, consult the website.

Birky Family Farms Country Market

PORK

506 South SR 49, Valparaiso IN 46383 (Porter)
219-766-3270 • www.birkyfarms.com

Jake and Emma Birky established their Porter County farm in 1919. Now the third generation of Birkys is leading the operation. They have built a reputation for offering high-quality pork raised with, as they put it, "no antibiotics, no growth hormones, no animal by-products, and no bull!" Their convenient Country Market features a wonderful selection of their products, including meaty ribs, thick-cut pork chops, a staggering variety of sausages, lean hot dogs, tenderloins, country bacon, smoked hams, pork steaks, and pork burgers. A Pork Patty Wagon provides catering and onsite grilling for events. Their products can also be ordered online. Call for market hours.

Blackjack's Poultry Farm

CHICKEN, EGGS

> 4455 South SR 39, North Judson IN 46366 (Starke)
> 219-742-6783

Blackjack chickens lead happy lives. They have plenty of room to roam, with lots of sunshine and fresh air, are fed an all-natural diet, and are not dosed with antibiotics or other chemicals. We should all be so lucky! Tony Kaminski runs Blackjack's, and his customers say that his birds are the juiciest, most delicious in the area. He sells whole chickens and cut-up parts. He takes special orders for Thanksgiving turkeys, and he has chicken eggs year-round. Blackjack poultry can be ordered directly from Kaminski, and Au Naturel Market, at 1708 Lincoln Way in Valparaiso, carries his birds in the frozen foods section.

Blue Sky Berry Farm

BLUEBERRIES

> 15552 S. 1050 W., Wanatah IN 46390 (LaPorte)
> 219-733-2416 • www.blueskyberryfarm.com

Lew and Jennifer Van Meter were looking for a home to buy in Wanatah and, while searching online, they found a farmhouse for sale that also included a blueberry farm.

"Hey, we like blueberries. How about this?" The rest, as they say, is history. The Van Meters have made Blue Sky Berry Farm a family destination offering a picnic shelter, a playground, lawn games, and public restrooms. They offer both U-Pick and Ready-Pick blueberries throughout the month of July. They also sell jam, no-sugar-added fruit spread, and syrup, all made from their own berries. Call for hours of operation.

Broken Wagon Bison

BISON

> 563 W. 450 N., Hobart IN 46342 (Lake)
> 219-759-3523

Brothers Bud and Wally Koeppen, along with Bud's wife Ruth, began operating Broken Wagon Bison in 2003 when Bud turned his passion for wildlife rehabilitation (he is a self-proclaimed Ellie Mae Clampett) into a bison business. When it came time to name the enterprise, they looked no father than the broken-down wagon in the barn. They now offer a wide variety of bison products, including steaks, patties, ground meat, canned meat, and jerky. They welcome visitors but hours vary, so calling ahead is recommended. You can also find a Broken Wagon Bison Burger on the menu at Suzie's Café and Catering in Valparaiso (p. 38).

Crème de la Crop

PRODUCE

> 208 N. 250 W., Valparaiso IN 46385 (Porter)
> 219-510-4547 • www.cremedelacrop.com

Crème de la Crop searches internationally for rare organic and heirloom seeds from which to grow produce. Leann Landgrebe Stephens plants more than 10 acres and more than 200 varieties of vegetables, fruits, and herbs. The farm is chemical-free and uses organic methods, biodynamic principles, and the latest scientific techniques. Crème de la Crop sells its produce at its farm stand on Wednesdays and Fridays and on Saturdays at the Valparaiso Farmers' Market. Most sales, however, are to subscribers to the farm's Community Supported Agriculture (CSA) program. More information about this program is available on the website. (Also see "What Is a CSA?" on p. 180.)

Farm Direct Meat

PORK, BEEF, LAMB, CHICKEN, BISON, PHEASANT

St. John IN 46373 (Lake)
866-495-9133 • www.farmdirectmeat.com

Farm Direct Meat is a retail distributor of locally farmed, naturally raised meat. It partners only with small family farmers who pledge not to feed their animals growth hormones or antibiotics. It offers meats from animals raised humanely, with plenty of room and access to the outdoors. It also sells some premium products, such as dry-aged beef and hard-to-find cuts. It sells and delivers whole-, half-, and quarter-animal orders to the Chicago metro area, Indiana, and western Michigan. Individual cuts are sold at several area farmers' markets. Orders can also be placed online.

J n J Organic Farm

HEIRLOOM TOMATOES

489 E. 500 S., Kouts IN 46347 (Porter)
219-462-6727

Names like Aunt Ginny's Purple, Boxcar Willie, and German Johnson sound like they belong on a vaudeville playbill, but, fortunately for hungry shoppers in northwest Indiana, they are really the names of some of the heirloom tomatoes available at Andy and Gail Vasquez's J n J Organic Farm. J n J has garnered a reputation for offering one of the most extensive selections of organic heirloom tomatoes in the tri-state area. When you buy a J n J tomato you know that it was picked the night before or maybe even that very morning. The Vasquez's produce can be found at the farmers' markets in Crown Point and Valparaiso.

Kohlhagen Asparagus

ASPARAGUS

3653 N. 700 W., Rensselaer IN 47978 (Jasper)
219-866-3279

Richard and Carol Kohlhagen are busy people from about April 20 until June 5 of each year—so busy, in fact, that their grown kids return home to help out when they can. During the growing season, new plants reach the eight-inch harvesting height every day on their 15-acre farm. Each stalk gets snapped off at the ground by hand, and on some days the Kohlhagens need to harvest twice. They sell their produce to grocery stores across the state, and folks from the region show up at the farm to purchase it by the pound. Customers can call ahead and their order will be ready to pick up.

Laney Honey

HONEY

> 25725 New Rd., North Liberty IN 46554 (St. Joseph)
> 574-656-8701 • www.laneyhoney.com

What began as a hobby for Dave Laney in the 1970s has evolved into a thriving family business with a staggering array of honey varieties. Rather than mixing all of the honeys together under one label, Laney separates them by floral source. Laney Honey has grown its product line to include plenty of honeys from right here in the Midwest and two imports: Orange Blossom, from Florida, and Wild Blackberry, from British Columbia. Its products can be found in many Indiana grocery stores, usually in their own wooden-shelved display. Honey can also be ordered online.

LE Garden

PRODUCE

> 16521 N. 550 W., Wheatfield IN 46392 (Jasper)
> 219-987-6634

The LE in LE Garden stands for Linda Ebert. She and her husband Ron began farming their 10 acres in 1997. They specialize in peppers, tomatoes, and eggplants, but they have also grown asparagus, okra, cucumbers, winter and summer squash, potatoes, sweet potatoes, broccoli, cabbage, kohlrabi, and many more. They sell their produce through a Community Supported Agriculture (CSA) program and have drop-off sites in Valparaiso, Crown Point, and Miller. Members can buy full shares, which will feed three to four people, or half shares, for one to two, and receive produce weekly from late May though early October. (See "What Is a CSA?" on p. 180)

Old World Market

PRODUCE, GOURMET FOODS, WINE

> 76 S. Washington St., Valparaiso IN 46383 (Porter)
> 219-476-0700 • www.oldworldmarketonline.com

Since 2000, Dee and John Kowalski have been bringing great food and wine from around the world to shoppers in downtown Valparaiso. In 2007, after attending a local foods expo, they decided to add local produce to their product line. The Valparaiso Farmers' Market brings local fruit and vegetable vendors downtown on Saturdays, but during the rest of the week there used to be few places to obtain locally grown produce. The Old World Market changed all that; customers can now pick up local fruits and vegetables at the same time they purchase imported cheeses, 90-point wines, and other culinary delights. The Market is open Tuesdays through Fridays from 10:00 AM to 6:00 PM and Saturdays from 10:00 AM to 5:00 PM.

Oscar Nemeth

EGGS (CHICKEN, DUCK, GOOSE).
HUNGARIAN PASTRIES AND NOODLES

> 4800 SR 40, North Liberty IN 46554 (St. Joseph)
> 574-656-8780

For more than 35 years, Oscar Nemeth has sold his eggs at the South Bend Farmers' Market. And what he brings in, from his North Liberty farm, are not run-of-the-mill eggs. Sure, there's the chicken variety, but he also offers also duck and goose eggs. In addition, he sells Hungarian pastries and egg noodles, made in the Old World style. The pastries are flakey and butter-rich, and the noodles come in thin, medium, and wide. Nemeth is a fixture at the market, and a whole host of regular customers look to him to satisfy their sweet tooth and to keep them stocked up on eggs for the week.

Prairie Hills Bison Farm

BISON

5899 E. 1000 N., LaPorte IN 46350 (LaPorte)
219-778-9058 • prhbison@csinet.net

In the late 1990s Christopher and Lisa Beck decided they wanted an alternative red meat that was healthier than beef, so they started raising bison for their own family's consumption. They began with four pregnant cows, and a few years later they have a herd of 27 animals and sell to the general public. Although their bison can be found on the menu of some fine dining establishments (such as Kelly's Table; see p. 19), they sell most of their meat directly to consumers from their on-farm shop. They don't keep regular shop hours, so they are open by chance or by appointment. Give them a call or drop them an email to arrange a time to come by.

Pressel Strawberries

STRAWBERRIES

611 E. 400 S., Valparaiso IN 46383 (Porter)
219-733-2304

Several years ago, crop farmer Donald Pressel added a few acres of strawberries to earn a little extra income in the time between his corn, soybean, and wheat harvests. Northwest Indiana strawberry lovers are glad he did. The Pressels grow five different varieties in their U-Pick operation, and on their busiest days they can sell as many as 300 quarts of berries. Those interested in more details about the Pressels' farm should give them a call.

reverie

BIODYNAMIC DINNERS

> 3634 N. 700 W., LaPorte IN 46350 (Laporte)
> 219-861-0814 • www.spareverie.com

The reverie spa treats both the inside and outside of your body. It offers all the standard services: massage, facials, manicures and pedicures, and full-body slathering and wrapping in things like mud and seaweed. You can even stay overnight or all weekend in one of the luxuriously appointed rooms. The internal treatment comes into play in the meals prepared for guests. Behind reverie's 1890 Prairie-style farmhouse is an organic, biodynamic garden tended by Daniel Fagerstrom (a.k.a. "Organic Dan") of Fairstream Farms. Meals are prepared using the garden's bountiful produce. For the spa's meat, fish, and dairy offerings, the staff bring in fresh, quality ingredients. More information about all reverie's services can be found on its website.

Super Foods

GAME

> 141 N. Washington St., La Crosse IN 46348 (LaPorte)
> 219-754-2504

Lots of people are content to include only a limited number of animals in their diet—cows, pigs, chickens, turkeys, a few water creatures. To others, nearly any creature walking, crawling, swimming, or slithering is fair game.

For those interested in taking a somewhat bigger bite out of the animal kingdom, Super Foods in La Crosse is a great place to check out. This small-town grocery store has the largest selection of game in the state. Much of the game comes from Indiana, but not all. Looking for turtle, bear, or rattlesnake? Super Foods is the place to go. We wonder if they sold much bear during the 2007 Super Bowl?

Terra Spice Company

SPICES

605 Roosevelt Rd., Walkerton IN 46574 (Porter)
574-586-2600 • www.terraspice.com

Walkerton (pop. 2,274) is an unlikely place for a world-class spice house, but that is where Philip Abbot chose to settle his family and start Terra Spice Company. His primary customers are chefs—some of the best in the world. He gathers the highest-quality raw materials from around the world and uses his apothecary-like skills to crush, extract, and mix them to create his products. Although he does not sell directly to the public, Abbot has developed 70 different spice blends for retail, which are available at Cooking with Class (1225 E. University Dr. in Granger, 219-243-2665) and The Regal Rabbit (206 S. Calumet Rd. in Chesterton, 219-395-8814).

Wappel Farms

MINT

6235 S. 775 W., San Pierre IN 46374 (Starke)
574-896-3030 • www.mint-oil.com

There was a time, a few decades ago, when Indiana was

the top mint-producing state in the country. The essential oils were extracted in the many mint stills that dotted the northern part of the state. Companies like Chicago-based Wrigley looked across the state border to Indiana to flavor their chewing gum. Although no longer the number one producer, Indiana is still a fresh-breathed player in the mint business and quite a bit of mint is still grown and processed here. One producer is Larry Wappel, with more than 1,000 acres and an onsite mint distillery. The oils he extracts are distributed all over the world. There's a good chance that stick of Wrigley's chewing gum in your mouth is flavored with some of his top-rate mint oil. Wappel Farms also sells its bottled mint oil directly to consumers through its website. The Wappels enjoy visitors during the summer months, when their products are available onsite. Call to make arrangements for a farm visit.

PASTURED POULTRY AND EGGS

In the simpler past, food choices were much more clear-cut than they are now. A chicken was a chicken. If you stop by the supermarket today, however, you may see lots of different kinds of chicken. Labels like "all-natural," "free-range," "grain-fed," "no hormones administered," and "minimally processed," sometimes in dizzying combinations, keep some consumers guessing (and confused) about what sort of bird is best.

Despite the number of labels, there's actually not much variety in who is responsible for bringing that poultry to the store. The chicken industry is dominated by a handful of giant poultry companies that mass-produce birds for both retail sale and the food service industry. These large-scale operations have resulted in inexpensive, readily available poultry. What was once a splurge for Sunday dinner has become an everyday expectation.

For a small but growing segment of the chicken-eating public, however, cheapness and availability are not the primary criteria for poultry and eggs. An increasing number of shoppers are asking questions about animal welfare, chemicals and additives used in feed, and flavor, but the labels don't necessarily tell them what they want to know. Some, like "cage-free," don't have any legal meaning at all, and others, like those using the word "natural," refer to how the bird was processed (e.g., without additives) rather than how it was raised. So how can a conscientious chicken shopper know what he or she is buying?

"Organic," when used in reference to poultry and eggs, means that the chickens were fed food meeting the legal definition of "organic" (see p. 100) and were not given drugs. A bird that is not organic may still be "drug-free," meaning that it was not given the antibiotics typically fed to mass-produced birds to prevent infection. Growth hormones are not given to chickens in the United States. Studies have shown that they do not increase the birds' size and the USDA has banned their use, so claims that a chicken is hormone-free are a bit like Seven-Up's claim to be non-caffeinated: it couldn't be anything else.

"Free-range" sounds like a quaint description of chickens freely roaming the great outdoors, but according to the USDA it just means the chicken had "access" to the great outdoors for 51 percent of its life, not necessarily that it took advantage of that access. A free-range chicken's cage might have a door to the outside, but frequently that door is kept shut during its youth to prevent infections that the manufacturer cannot treat without losing the ability to claim that it is drug-free. By the time the door is unlatched, the chicken has learned to stay indoors and may never go outside. Still, the label reads "free-range," sending confusing signals about how the bird was raised.

Many consumers who want chickens that actually got to live as they used to are turning to farmers like Joel Salatin of Virginia (polyfacefarms.com) and his many converts, including some right here in Indiana. (See, for example, Apple Family Farm, p. 110; Rhodes Family Farm, p. 178; and Skillington Farms, p. 130.) Their "pastured" chickens are raised in the field—hunting and pecking on the ground, eating plants, bugs, and whatever else they can find. Salatin pastures his chickens on fields that have just been grazed by cows. The chickens' search for delectable bugs helps break down the cow manure and convert it to nutrients that help build up the soil and allow the grass to grow back lushly; meanwhile the chickens get fat and happy.

Taste is perhaps the largest reason people turn to pastured poultry and the resulting eggs. Birds that get to forage for the majority of their food taste more like chicken used to taste; modern flavor enhancers like brining are not necessary when preparing pastured chicken. On the other hand, truly free-range chickens, which have the opportunity to give their muscles a workout, can be not only more flavorful but also tougher than the ones whose movements are restricted, suiting them for a long slow braise. The eggs of pastured chickens typically have yolks of a deeper, richer yellow and are more flavorful as well. They can be a taste revelation to someone raised on the anemic supermarket version.

There are lots of nuances to chicken-buying, just as there are to buying other foods. One way to cut through all the mumbo jumbo is to decide which factors are most important to you—do you want your food to be local, to be organic, to come from well-treated animals, or to combine these and other considerations? The virtue of buying local is that you get to talk to farmers, visit the farms, ask questions, and make up your own mind.

EATING LOCAL WHILE DINING OUT

Bistro 157
157 Lincoln Way, Valparaiso IN 46383 (Porter)
219-462-0992 • www.bistro157.net

Corndance Café
117 S. Main St., Culver IN 46511 (Marshall)
574-842-3220 • www.corndance.com

Dish Restaurant
3907 N. Calumet Ave., Valparaiso IN 46383 (Porter)
219-465-9221

Kelly's Table at Creekwood Inn
5727 N. 600 W., Michigan City IN 46360 (LaPorte)
219-872-5624 • www.kellyscreekwood.com
See p. 19

Maria Elena's Restaurant
454 S. Greenwich St., Valparaiso IN 46383 (Porter)
219-477-2490

Marilyn's Bakery and Dinner on the Terrace
8960 E. Ridge Rd., Hobart IN 46342 (Lake)
219-962-BAKE (2253) • www.marilynsbakery.com
See p. 21

Moser's Café and Catering
127 E. Michigan St., New Carlisle IN 46552 (St. Joseph)
574-654-8466 • www.moserscafe.net

Pier 74 Pizza Grill
13125 N.E. Lake Shore Dr., Cedar Lake IN 46303 (Porter)
219-374-7474 • www.pier74pizza.com

Suzie's Café and Catering
1050 Southpoint Circle, Valparaiso IN 46385 (Porter)
219-462-5500 • www.suziescafeandcatering.com

Three Floyds Brew Pub
9570 Indiana Pkwy., Munster IN 46321 (Porter)
219-922-4425 • www.threefloydspub.com

Victorian Pantry Bistro & Catering
226 W. Cleveland Rd., Granger IN 46530 (St. Joseph)
574-271-7881 • www.victorianpantry.com

FARMERS' MARKETS

Chesterton's European Market
Corner of Broadway and 3rd Streets
Chesterton IN 46304 (Porter)
May–October, Saturdays 8:00 AM to 2:00 PM
www.chestertonseuropeanmarket.com

Crown Point Farmers' Market
101 N. East St., Crown Point IN 46307 (Lake)
June–September, Saturdays 7:00 AM to 12 noon

Griffith Farmers' Market
1532 E. Main St., Griffith IN 46319 (Lake)
June–October, Tuesdays 4:00 to 8:00 PM

Highland Community Street Market
Corner of Kennedy and Highway Avenues
Highland IN 46322 (Lake)
June–October, Saturdays 9:00 AM to 1:00 PM

LaPorte Farmers' Market
State St., north of the courthouse
LaPorte IN 46350 (LaPorte)
May–October, Saturdays 7:00 AM to 12 noon

Michigan City Farmers' Market
Corner of 8th and Washington Streets
Michigan City IN 46360 (LaPorte)
May–October, Saturdays 8:00 AM to 12 noon
www.mcmainstreet.com

Rensselaer Farmers' Market
115 W. Washington St., Rensselaer IN 47978 (Jasper)
May–October, Saturdays 7:00 to 11:00 AM

St. John Farmers' Market
9660 Wicker Ave., St. John IN 46373 (Lake)
May–October, Sundays 8:00 AM to 1:00 PM

Schererville's International Market
1722 S. Park Ave., Schererville IN 46375 (Lake)
June 21–October 25, 2nd and 4th Thursdays 3:00 to 8:00 PM

South Bend Farmers' Market
1165 North Side Blvd., South Bend IN 46615 (St. Joseph)
Open year-round, Tuesdays and Thursdays 7:00 AM
    to 2:00 PM; May–September, Fridays 7:00 AM
    to 2:00 PM; Saturdays 7:00 AM to 3:00 PM
www.southbendfarmersmarket.com

Valparaiso Farmers' Market
16 Lincoln Way, Valparaiso IN 46383 (Porter)
May–October, Saturdays (May) 8:00 AM to 2:00 PM
Saturdays, Tuesdays, and Thursdays (June–
    October) 8:00 AM to 2:00 PM

Whiting Farmers' Market
1443 119th St., Whiting IN 46394 (Lake)
June–October, Fridays 8:00 AM to 2:00 PM

Winfield Farmer-Family-Friends Market
10645 Randolph St., Winfield IN 46341 (Lake)
June–September, Saturdays 8:30 AM to 12 noon

WINERIES

Anderson's Orchard and Winery
430 East US 6, Valparaiso IN 46383 (Porter)
219-464-4936

Lake Michigan Winery
816 119th St., Whiting IN 46394 (Lake)
219-659-WINE (9463) • www.lakemichiganwinery.com

MICROBREWERIES & BREWPUBS

Back Road Brewery
1315 Michigan Ave., LaPorte IN 46350 (LaPorte)
219-362-7623 • www.backroadbrewery.com

Mishawaka Brewing
3703 N. Main St., Mishawaka IN 46545 (St. Joseph)
574-256-9993 • www.mishawakabrewingcompany.com

Shoreline Brewery
208 Wabash St., Michigan City IN 46360 (LaPorte)
219-879-4677 • www.shorelinebrewery.com

Three Floyds Brewing
9750 Indiana Pkwy., Munster IN 46321 (Lake)
219-922-3565 • www.threefloyds.com

FOOD FESTIVALS

Annual Heirloom Tomato Fest
Tomato tasting, salsa contest, and lots of food
Michigan City IN (LaPorte)
Mid-August
219-871-0140

Kouts Pork Fest
Grilling contest and plenty to eat
Kouts IN (Porter)
End of August
219-766-2867 • www.kouts.org

Maple Syrup Time at Deep River
Hobart IN (Lake)
Demonstration of maple syrup making, from tapping trees to tasting
1st and 2nd weekends in March
219-769-7275 • www.lakecountyparks.org

Marshall County Blueberry Festival
Blueberries and blueberry treats
Plymouth IN (Marshall)
Early September
888-936-5020 • www.blueberryfestival.org

Northwest Indiana

Mint Festival
Mint still tours and all things mint
North Judson IN (Starke)
Mid-June (always on Father's Day)
574-896-5481 • www.explorestarkecounty.com

Pierogi Festival
Whiting IN (Lake)
Pierogis, a pierogi-tossing contest, and Mr. Pierogi
End of July
877-659-0292 • www.pierogifest.net

Valparaiso Popcorn Festival
Popcorn and the nation's only popcorn parade
Valparaiso IN (Porter)
Early September
219-464-8332 • www.popcornfest.org

44

Elkhart Lagrange Steuben
Noble De Kalb
NORTHEAST
Whitley Allen
Fulton
Wabash Huntington
Wells Adams

Northeast

Snuggled up against the Michigan and Ohio borders, northeast Indiana offers some delightful options for local flavor, including the Midwest's largest farmers' market. This region is anchored by Fort Wayne, Indiana's second-largest city, with a thriving grocery co-op and farm stands that have served multiple generations. Northeast Indiana is also home to the country's third-largest largest Amish and Mennonite communities. Their straightforward style of cooking can be enjoyed in several restaurants in the region, and their largely agrarian culture makes for abundant produce, meats, and baked goods. LaGrange and Nappanee are popular tourist destinations but also have plenty to offer the locals.

The region has some unexpected food finds, like authentic Swiss-style cheeses in Swiss-settled Berne, and Kobe-style beef (first raised in Japan) in Roanoke. The region is also home to Indiana's only pickle festival. Two grain mills that are more than 100 years old add to the region's distinction. Both of these mills produce flours and baking mixes, including some organic offerings. Northwest Indiana has much to see—plenty, even, for an overnight stay.

American Countryside Farmers' Market

PRODUCE, MEATS, CHEESE, AND DINING COURT

27751 CR 26, Elkhart IN 46517 (Elkhart)
574-296-7827 • www.americancountryside.us

Home Grown Indiana

The American Countryside Farmers' Market is a remarkable site to behold—51,000 square feet of fresh produce, meats, baked goods, fresh flowers, and a food court. In addition to the food, local craftspeople and artisans sell their wares—heritage-quality furniture, candles, stained glass, and sculptures. The structure itself is amazing—the Amish-built wood-peg structure is the largest building of its type in the world. It cost $4.5 million to construct, sits on 15 acres, and is home to the largest farmers' market in the Midwest.

The market grew from the collective vision of four local men—farmer Kenny BeMiller, architect LeRoy Troyer, developer and builder Art Moser, and attorney Mick Tuesley. It opened in May of 2007 and has space for a staggering 493 vendors—215 inside, 41 on the facilities porch, and 237 seasonal outdoor vendors. Although some vendors come from nearby Michigan and Ohio, most are from northeast Indiana. Vendors sell a range of local goods, including fruits, vegetables, meats, and cheeses. Some sell foods typical of Amish country—kettle corn, handmade candies, spices, fresh-baked breads, and homestyle noodles.

In addition to many vendors of food-related products, the first floor also features an extensive food court that blends the convenience of a suburban shopping mall with Amish-country choices. Among the foods available are burgers made of naturally raised, locally grown beef and buffalo, salads made with as much local produce as possible, all-natural rotisserie chicken, sirloin tips, and apple fritters. The market's founders aim to celebrate the area's cultural heritage, and toward that end you will also find foods reflecting Polish, Greek, Italian, Asian, Hispanic, and African-American roots.

The market maintains a festival-like atmosphere and offers many activities to enjoy while you visit. Kids love the petting zoo and pony rides, and musicians serenade shoppers and diners. The second floor features a state-of-the-art demonstration kitchen which is under the culinary leadership of the market's own food specialist. The kitchen is used for cooking classes, competitions, and demonstrations by guest cooks and chefs of local, regional, and national fame.

The demonstration kitchen is just one component of the market's focus on education. Vendors, as well as staff, are knowledgeable and conversant. Walking through the market talking with folks can provide a crash course in nutrition, agri-science, economics, craft work and furniture making, and the cultures of several ethnic groups.

The American Countryside Farmers' Market represents a grand experiment. Nothing else quite like it exists. We're fortunate, in Indiana, to be the beneficiaries of this innovative enterprise. The market is open year-round on Thursdays, Fridays, and Saturdays from 7:00 AM to 3:30 PM. Check the website for more information about special events held throughout the year.

Indigo on 17

RESTAURANT

56039 Parkway Ave., Elkhart IN 46516 (Elkhart)
574-293-1717 • www.indigoon17.com

Executive chef Kelly Graff and general manager Karen Kennedy established themselves distinctively in the Indiana culinary landscape with their earlier restaurant, Citrus at the Checkerberry Inn. Their August 2007 opening of Indigo on 17 was greatly anticipated by their loyal followers and it piqued the curiosity of others, some of whom seemed amazed that a new restaurant was not part of a national chain. But everything at Graff and Kennedy's place is local—the art on the walls is by local artists, the nightly jazz is played by area musicians, and the in-season produce is grown by local farmers.

They describe their menu as "American cuisine jazzed with flavors of Asia and the Caribbean." This fusion of the heartland with more exotic flavors is an extension of Graff's life. She splits her time between Indiana and the Caribbean island of Anguilla, where she grew up. Chef Graff has an impressive list of celebrities in her fan club. Actress Liv Tyler, actor Steve Buscemi, Indianapolis Colts owner Jim Ersay, and Chicago mayor Richard Daley are among her devotees. And Kennedy's 20-plus years of restaurant management show in her attention to detail as she looks after the front of the house. She was a singer before entering the restaurant business, and she sometimes finds her way to the stage to do some entertaining herself.

The dinner menu at Indigo on 17 includes several soups, an impressive selection of small plates, a couple of salads, and entrées that cover all the basics—beef, seafood, poultry, vegetarian—including Graff's signature Wasabi-Pea-Encrusted Salmon with Soy Ginger Glaze. And there are ten or more options for a sweet ending to the meal.

Indigo on 17 is open for lunch Mondays through Fridays from 11:00 AM to 2:00 PM, and for dinner Mondays through Thursdays from 5:30 PM to 10:00 PM and Fridays and Saturdays from 5:30 PM to 11:00 PM. Sample menus are available online.

ASIAN WRAP SALAD WITH
PASSIONFRUIT VINAIGRETTE

Chef Kelly Graf uses fresh organic produce from Sustainable Greens (264-244-8355) in nearby Jones, Michigan, and exotic flavors from across the globe to create these Asian-inspired spring roll–like wraps.

Passionfruit Vinaigrette

- · 1 cup passionfruit purée
- · 2 cloves garlic
- · 1 whole shallot
- · ½ teaspoon salt
- · ½ teaspoon pepper
- · ½ cup red wine vinegar
- · 1 tablespoon Indiana honey
- · 1½ cups extra-virgin olive oil

Asian Salad

- · 8 sheets rice paper
- · Rice wine vinegar, for soaking rice paper
- · 1 pound locally grown organic arugula
- · 1 locally grown organic daikon radish, julienned
- · ¼ cup locally grown fresh purple basil, chopped
- · ½ mango, sliced
- · 1 avocado, sliced
- · 1 cup sliced, toasted almonds

In a food processor blend the passionfruit purée, garlic, shallot, salt, pepper, vinegar, and honey. Slowly add the olive oil and blend until thoroughly mixed. Set aside.

Take one sheet of rice paper, soak it in rice wine vinegar until soft and pliable, and lay it flat on a plate. Mix the arugula, radish, and basil in a small bowl and toss with vinaigrette. Spread ⅛ of the dressed vegetables in a long row along the center of the rice paper, fanning out at the top. Next, fan

Northeast Indiana

the mango and avocado out toward the top. Roll into a cone and drizzle with additional vinaigrette. Finish with the almonds. Repeat process with remaining ingredients. Serves 8.

Joseph Decuis Restaurant and Heritage Farm

BEEF, RESTAURANT

> 191 N. Main St., Roanoke IN 46783 (Huntington)
> 260-672-1715 • www.josephdecuis.com

As one of Indiana's consistently top-rated restaurants, Joseph Decuis attends to every detail of a dining experience. Proprietor Alice Eshelman and her staff are committed to using the best ingredients in their menu. Sometimes that means searching far and wide, but they are increasingly turning to sources much closer to home. The garden behind the restaurant provides in-season herbs and vegetables, and in the off-season they use locally grown hydroponic tomatoes. On the restaurant's Heritage Farm, they raise chickens, turkey, and eggs, and in 2007 they took the Indiana culinary world by storm by adding Kobe-style beef to the farm's animal population.

Beef from the Kobe region of Japan began creating a stir among elite Western food experts and aficionados in the mid-1990s. Stories of how the cattle were raised seemed outrageous—the animals were given daily massages and a diet that included beer. Fascination with Kobe beef grew, and a staggering number of people began paying prices of well over $100 per pound for this Japanese delicacy.

It did not take long for the American entrepreneurial spirit to take over and Kobe beef started being raised here in the U.S. As it turned out, the secret was not in the beer and massages, but in the basic genetics of the breed of cattle—Wagyu. This type of cow is an anomaly among cattle; its meat is much more marbled than that of other breeds and has a higher ratio of monosaturated fats to saturated fats. Some claim that it also has high levels of omega-3 and omega-6 fatty acids. Amazingly, this is not only some of the most delicious beef in existence, but may also be some of the healthiest.

In 2003, Joseph Decuis put Kobe on the menu and it was an immediate hit with the patrons. Eshelman and her staff set out to learn more about the breed. They met and became friends with the handful of people who were pioneering Kobe-style beef in the U.S., and set their sights on raising the cattle themselves on their Heritage Farm, located just six miles from the restaurant. They acquired the finest breeding stock, consulted with the experts, and began raising cattle in a healthy, drug-free, stress-free environment. The calves born at the Heritage Farm are part Angus and part Wagyu, and the mix produces robust beef that maintains the Kobe tenderness.

The farm now supplies all the restaurant's Kobe-style beef, making Joseph Decuis the only establishment in Indiana, and perhaps the Midwest, serving home-grown American Kobe-style beef. Not only is the meat served at the restaurant, it is also sold directly to the customer at the Emporium, located next door. Since there is no middleman, prices are much lower than you would find nearly anywhere else. Joseph Decuis's beef is available in halves or in individual cuts. A half will provide about 200 pounds of meat. The number of halves available is limited, so customers are encouraged to place orders in advance. Halves start becoming available each April. Individual cuts for purchase include filets, ribeyes, strip loins, and ground steak. Orders can be shipped anywhere in Indiana. The Emporium at Joseph Decuis is open Tuesdays through Saturdays from 10:00 AM to 7:00 PM. The restaurant is open Tuesdays through Saturdays as well, serving lunch from 11:30 AM to 2:00 PM and dinner from 5:30 to 10:00 PM. Call for reservations.

KOBE FILET MIGNON WITH
PINOT NOIR SAUCE

Joseph Decuis executive chef Aaron Butts has developed this and other can't-miss recipes for the restaurant's home-grown Kobe-style beef.

- · 4 Indiana Kobe-style filet mignons (6 ounces each)
- · Kosher salt and freshly ground black pepper
- · 6 tablespoons cold unsalted butter
- · 1 onion, thinly sliced
- · 1 tablespoon minced garlic
- · 1 bay leaf
- · ¼ cup tomato paste
- · 2½ cups good Pinot Noir

Preheat the grill to medium high. Generously season the steaks with salt and pepper. Grill to desired doneness, about 5 minutes per side for medium rare. Transfer the steaks to a cutting board and let stand 10 minutes.

Meanwhile, melt 2 tablespoons of butter in a large, heavy saucepan over medium-high heat. Add the onions and sauté until tender, about 5 minutes. Season with salt, add the garlic and bay leaf, and sauté until fragrant, about 30 seconds. Stir in the tomato paste and cook for 2 minutes, stirring constantly. Now whisk in the wine. Simmer for about 10 minutes until the sauce reduces by half, stirring occasionally. Remove the saucepan from the heat. Strain the sauce into a small bowl, pressing on the solids to extract as much liquid as possible. Discard the solids remaining in the strainer, return *the sauce to the saucepan, and bring it to a slow simmer. Cut the remaining 4 tablespoons of butter into 1/2-inch chunks and whisk into the sauce a little at a time. Season the sauce to taste with salt and pepper. Serve the filets with the sauce alongside. Serves 4.*

3 Rivers Co-op Natural Food & Deli

MEMBER-OWNED CO-OP

1612 Sherman Blvd., Fort Wayne IN 46808 (Allen)
260-424-8812 • www.3riversfood.coop

In the 1970s about 200 people got together to form a natural foods buying club. They ordered food collectively each month and all pitched in to help gather and distribute it. After a couple of years, the club's members decided to open up a retail store. The 3 Rivers Food Co-op opened its doors to the public on October 1, 1976. Members volunteered as both management and staff. Over the years, the store outgrew its original location; membership swelled and the volunteer staff couldn't keep up with the increasingly complex organization. Today, the co-op has more than 1,900 members with professional management and a paid staff of 50. Anyone can join for a low annual fee, and members save five percent off the prices charged to the general public. Volunteers continue to be an important part of the operation, helping to augment staff and keep prices low. For their work, volunteers save an additional five percent on their purchases.

The product line has grown as the store has expanded. In the beginning, the co-op had a couple of coolers and a few shelves. It now carries a full line of fresh organic produce, natural groceries, dairy products, bulk foods, baked goods, fresh deli and café food, frozen foods, vitamins and supplements, natural body care products, and books and other educational materials. In the produce and dairy sections, local products are clearly labeled. Milk and cheeses from Traders Point Creamery in Zionsville are popular choices, as are eggs from local farms. There is no fresh meat counter but there is a selection of frozen meats, including beef, pork, chicken, buffalo, and more, many from familiar Indiana producers and a few from across the border in Michigan.

Many of the amenities found in upscale grocery stores are available in the 3 Rivers Co-op, including a coffee shop and café. While shopping, you can enjoy a latte made with fair-trade espresso beans and organic milk, or a smoothie made with organic fruits and yogurt. If you're there at mealtime, you can grab a bite at the Old World Café, where you can choose among deli sandwiches, paninis, and soups, or serve yourself from the hot entrée and salad bars, which offer a variety of seasonal options.

The 3 Rivers Co-op is more than a grocery store. It serves as a community hub for those interested in whole foods, health and wellness, and even the arts. It hosts educational seminars, poetry readings, live music, and more. Members benefit from even more services, including a monthly newsletter. The 3 Rivers Co-op is open Mondays through Saturdays from 7:00 AM to 9:00 PM and Sundays from 10:00 AM to 6:00 PM.

Wilmot Mill

ORGANIC GRAINS AND BAKING MIXES

2978 South SR 5-57, Pierceton IN 46562 (Kosciusko)
800-387-1804 • www.wilmotmill.com

The story of Wilmot Mill goes all the way back to 1840, when Jacob Ryder built a dam and a water-powered saw mill and grist mill. The Ryders operated the mill for years, until it burned to the ground in the 1930s. In 1939 a barn from the original homestead was converted to a feed mill that was operated for almost 40 years, powered first by an underwater turbine and then by gasoline. When the feed mill closed its doors, the structure fell into disrepair. In the early 1980s two retired schoolteachers, Pat and Walt Johnson, purchased the property and refurbished the original mill timber by timber and piece by piece.

While operating the mill, Pat Johnson compiled recipes for her *Old Mill Cookbook*. In the preface she writes,

> Old mill history survives because people love
> old mills. The romance of age makes the tinkle of
> water over the old wheels a piper's call to those
> who admire the courage of pioneers that survived
> the wilderness and made it produce. The surge of
> water and the groan of the wheel revive memories
> of a brave people wresting the land from swamp
> and forest to raise families on the fruit of that land.
> Wilmot Mill is a part of those dreams for it was
> built before the land was cleared or the forest gone
> from Northern Indiana.

In 1996, the Johnsons decided to get out of the mill business and sold the operation to Howard and Karen Luehrs. The Luehrses now run the mill according to the same philosophy by which they raised their children: "Do the right thing, be grateful for the many blessings we enjoy, and have fun." The Wilmot Mill operates today much as it did in the early years—water borrowed from Wilmot Pond powers the water wheel and turns the 160-year-old buhr stones to slow-grind the grains.

Wilmot Mill uses only organic grains, and grinding them slowly helps preserve their nutrients. The products available depend on what grains the Luehrses have procured, but they usually include baking mixes, breakfast cereals, and five different all-natural pancake mixes— Amaizing, Buckwheat, Buttermilk, Multigrain, and Pecan. All of them can be ordered through the Wilmot Mill website, as can Pat Johnson's *Old Mill Cookbook.*

Tours of Wilmot Mill are available throughout the year for groups of up to 100 people, except in the coldest of winter when the water wheel is frozen. Costs vary depending on the size of the group. The most popular tour is the Twisted Tour, which lasts for about one hour. It includes a hands-on demonstration of the milling process, and then everyone on the tour uses freshly ground flour to make hot pretzels. While the pretzels bake, the Luehrses are available to discuss the history of the mill, the various grains they use, and the difference between whole-grain and white flour. As a former science teacher, Howard Luehrs is a great tour guide for school groups and anyone interested in the physics of grinding and the healthfulness of grains. Call for more information.

Yoder Popcorn

POPCORN

> 7680 W. 200 S., Topeka IN 46571 (LaGrange)
> 260-768-4051 • www.yoderpopcorn.com

Go to any movie theater in the U.S. and chances are that that irresistible smell of popcorn is emanating from corn grown in Indiana, one of the top popcorn-producing states. Of course, the late superstar popcorn pitchman Orville Redenbacher helped put Indiana on the snack-food map, but there are several other big Indiana names in popcorn. Some companies, unlike Redenbacher's, have remained family-owned and are headquartered right here in the Hoosier state.

One of those great family businesses is Yoder Popcorn. The company's heritage dates all the way back to 1936, when Rufus Yoder started growing popcorn on the family farm. In the Amish way, he shared his excess crop with his friends and neighbors. Word spread as quickly as the aroma of popping corn, and soon demand was so high that what began as a fun sideline to the farming operation became its core business.

Members of the Yoder family continued to operate the business until it was sold in 1996. In 1999, a member of the Yoder family bought it back, and now the Yoders farm 1,700 acres and operate the Popcorn Shoppe at 7680 W. 200 S., about four miles south of Shipshewana. The shop is a popular destination for Amish Country tourists. The free samples are hard to resist, and they're certainly an effective marketing strategy—try, and you'll buy!

Yoder sells many varieties of popcorn, including White, Yellow, Lady Finger, Tiny Tinder, Red, Black, and Sunburst. All are available both at the shop and online, and most are offered in both standard and microwave-ready forms. Yoder also sells caramel corn. Both the store and the website sell everything else needed for the complete popcorn experience—oils, seasonings, and poppers.

Hoosiers are not the only ones to appreciate Yoder popcorn. Jane and Michael Stern, authors of more than 20 books (including *Roadfood* and *Eat Your Way across the USA*), recently named Yoder Popcorn as the best in the country during an interview on National Public Radio's program *The Splendid Table*.

The Yoders have spent a lot of time experimenting with their popcorn and offer more than 100 recipes on their website. Some are different from any popcorn you may ever have tasted. Viva Zapata, for example, gets its kick from cumin, oregano, and red pepper flakes. For a sweeter treat, they suggest a deliciously simple Maple Popcorn, flavored with maple syrup, butter, and vanilla. It would take more than two years of weekly family movie nights to make it through this extensive list.

Besides the website, Yoder's Popcorn Shoppe is the best bet for picking up their products. The shop is open Mondays through Fridays from 9:00 AM to 5:00 PM and Saturdays from 9:00 AM to 4:00 PM.

Amish Acres Restaurant Barn

RESTAURANT

1600 W. Market St., Nappanee IN 46550 (Elkhart)
800-800-4942 • www.amishacres.com

It's an understatement to say that the Thresher's Dinner served at the Amish Acres Historic Farm and Heritage Resort is popular. An estimated 120,000 people a year enjoy this traditional Amish dinner, served family-style in the Restaurant Barn. The menu offers a feast of choices— fried chicken, cider-baked ham, beef and noodles, and hearth-baked bread, along with a host of side dishes and desserts. There was a time when all the chicken and ham came from Indiana, but suppliers could not keep pace with the demand of 120,000 diners annually. Amish Acres does, however, still turn to local growers and producers for items like apple butter, honey, maple syrup, and its famous pickles. During the Thanksgiving season, turkeys come from nearby Indiana farms. Dinner is served Monday–Saturday and reservations are encouraged. See the website for more details.

Blue Gate Restaurant

RESTAURANT

105 E. Middlebury St., Shipshewana IN 46565 (LaGrange)
260-768-4725 • www.riegsecker.com

Like other Amish-style restaurants in this region of Indiana, Blue Gate Restaurant serves so many diners each day that it would be nearly impossible to source enough local ingredients. Still, when it can use local products, it does. The ground beef for the restaurant's hamburgers, for instance, comes from cattle both raised and processed in the area. Its extensive selection of pies includes some seasonal favorites like fresh blueberry and fresh peach, with fruit from nearby in Michigan. The restaurant serves breakfast, lunch, and dinner Monday through Saturday from 7:00 AM to 9:00 PM. Pies and other baked goods may be purchased in the restaurant bakery, which is open the same hours as the restaurant.

Broken Animal Inn

CHICKEN, RABBIT, PRODUCE

7901 South SR 9, Columbia City IN 46725 (Whitley)
260-385-8357 • www.brokenanimalinn.com

Broken Animal Inn is a family farm that also undertakes a mission of stewardship, working to preserve and propagate heritage-breed chickens, rescue and rehabilitate various breeds of barnyard animals, and restore and utilize old barns. The farm does not use herbicides, pesticides, or chemical fertilizers. Its products include heritage-breed chickens raised free of antibiotics, eggs from these free-range chickens, rabbits, and naturally grown produce and seeds for planting. All are sold directly from the farm.

Visitors are welcome. Call or check out the website for more information or to schedule a visit.

Bryr Patch

HERBS AND FLAVORED VINEGARS

> 2575 S. 800 E., Angola IN 46703 (Steuben)
> 260-668-4042 • www.bryrpatch.com

The folks at Bryr Patch specialize in herbs and herb-infused vinegars. To make their flavored vinegars, they pick herbs fresh and stuff into the jar as much herbal goodness as they can. They then fill the jar with vinegar and let it steep in the sun at least two weeks before straining and bottling it. Each bottle has a sprig or two of fresh herbs added as well. Varieties of vinegars include Thyme, Tarragon, Chive, Dill, Sage, and Rosemary, and Bryr Patch takes special requests. The farm also grows heirloom vegetables and sells organic brown eggs. Purchases can be made on the farm Mondays through Wednesdays, and Bryr Patch products are regularly available at Elkhart's American Countryside Farmers' Market.

Cairdeas Druim

BEEF

> 3790 W. 050 N., LaGrange IN 46761 (LaGrange)
> 260-463-2249 • www.hairycows.com

Cairdeas Druim Farm participates in the Quality Highland Beef program, the highland beef equivalent of the Good Housekeeping seal of approval, and its animals graze freely all summer on clean pasture that is free from herbicides and pesticides. In the winter they are fed high-quality hay, grown on the farm. Their all-natural beef is processed at the nearby Mishler Packing Company, and customers can choose how they would like it cut and packaged. Customers also have the option of having the animal delivered on the hoof directly to their door. Steers are usually fed grain for 60 days prior to market, but customers can request a strictly grass-fed animal. There is usually a waiting list for beef, so contact the farm well in advance.

Catalpa Farm

CHICKEN

> 5502 North SR 9, Columbia City IN 46725 (Whitley)
> 260-691-3468 • www.catalpafarmfresh.com

Catalpa Farm focuses on preserving heritage breeds, as designated by the American Livestock Breed Association. The farm has selected one of the most endangered breeds of chicken, the Delaware, to offer as an alternative to the breeds that are typically raised for meat. It is also developing breeding stock, to encourage other farmers to begin raising this bird again to save it from disappearing. Delawares take twice as long as modern chickens to come to full weight, which allows them to develop more fully. The result is chicken with a much richer taste than most standard poultry. You can find Catalpa Farm chicken at the Columbia City Farmers' Market.

Circle Dog Chicken Ranch

CHICKEN, TURKEY, HOT PEPPERS, EGGS

> 1631 South SR 5, Larwill IN 46764-9765 (Whitley)
> Kathy Adams • 877-411-7976

Kathy Graham Adams has more than 25 years' experience

as an organic gardener, and in 2001 she channeled this experience into operating Circle Dog Chicken Ranch. Her produce is grown without pesticides or herbicides, and compost is the main fertilizer. She also specializes in raising two rare heritage breeds of chickens, Buckeyes and Bantam Silkies, as well as raising turkeys, growing a variety of hot peppers, and selling free-range eggs. Adams loves to have people visit the ranch. Give her a call to inquire about how to purchase Circle Dog products or to arrange a visit.

Cook's Bison Ranch

BISON

5645 E. 600 S., Wolcottville IN 46795 (Noble)
866-382-2356 • www.cooksbisonranch.com

In 1939, Everett Cook invested $5,000 in 83 acres, with a house and a barn. Within two years he had a thriving popcorn-producing farm operation. In 1998, his grandson Pete inherited the farm. As a boy, Pete Cook had become fascinated with bison during a family trip to Wyoming. That fascination never waned, and when he took over the farm he decided that Wolcottville would become his home where the buffalo roam. He now operates a 900-acre bison ranch, with a herd of more than 300 animals. Cook's is a popular destination for group tours, which can include a hayride, hand-feeding the bison, and a bison-burger lunch. Call to arrange tours. Cook's products are available online.

Goshen Farmers' Market

MARKET, CSA

> 212 W. Washington St., PO Box 1031, Goshen IN 46526
> (Elkhart)
> 574-533-4747 • www.millrace.org

The Goshen Farmers' Market is a one-stop shop for fresh produce grown on the area's small family farms. Market vendors are local farmers and other community members who have joined together to support the local agricultural community. At the market you will find a broad array of local products, including fruits, vegetables, meats, cheese, honey and syrup, and lots more. Anyone can shop at the market, but the Community Sustainability Project, which organizes it, also offers a Community Supported Agriculture (CSA) program in which shareholders receive a weekly supply of farmers' market products (see "What Is a CSA?" on p. 180). The market is open year-round on Saturdays from 8:00 AM to 1:00 PM and on Tuesdays (May through October) from 3:00 to 7:00 PM.

Greenfield Mills

FLOURS AND BAKING MIXES

> 10505 E. 750 N., Howe IN 46747 (LaGrange)
> 260-367-2394 • www.newrinkelflour.com

Greenfield Mills has been owned and operated by the Rinkel family for more than 100 years. Located on the banks of the Fawn River, it is one of only a few water-powered mills left in the U.S. The mill not only grinds grain but also serves as Indiana's smallest electric utility company, powering two mills and 11 homes. Its product line includes bread and pastry flours (both white and whole wheat), some of them organic, as well as pancake mixes, breakfast cereals, and cornmeal. All are available at the

Northeast Indiana

onsite Old Mill Store, open Mondays through Fridays from 9:30 AM to 5:00 PM and Saturdays from 9:30 AM to 1:00 PM. Products can also be ordered online. Tours can be arranged by calling the Rinkels.

The Gunthorp's Farm

PORK AND CHICKEN

435 N. 850 E., LaGrange IN 46761 (LaGrange)
260-367-2708

Greg Gunthorp has built his farm a solid reputation as a provider of quality pork and poultry. He sells to high-end restaurants in Chicago and his poultry is a feature item at Goose the Market (p. 137) in Indianapolis. His animals are raised on pasture and they receive no antibiotics or growth stimulants. He sells chickens whole and in halves and split halves. Pork is available in chops, shoulder roasts, ground pork, bacon, and hams. Call Gunthorp for additional information and to learn other ways to get his products.

Hawkins Family Farm

PRODUCE, POULTRY, PORK, BEEF, EGGS

10373 N. 300 E., North Manchester IN 46962 (Wabash)
260-982-4961 • www.hawkinsfamilyfarm.com

Hawkins Family Farm is a one-stop CSA (Community Supported Agriculture) venture (see "What Is a CSA?" on p. 180). Shareholders get a wide variety of farm-fresh goods: produce during the growing season, pastured chickens, a fresh Thanksgiving turkey, pasture-raised pork, grass-fed beef, and free-range eggs. They also enjoy frequent surprise bonuses, like grapes from the farm's one vine and fresh-cut flowers. Home brewers, take note: the farm may soon offer barley and hops. Shares are usually sold out by June 1 of each year. Non-shareholders can still buy the farm's beef, pork, and poultry. See the website for more information.

Hilger's Friendly Market

PRODUCE

> 13210 US 30 W., Fort Wayne IN 46818 (Allen)
> www.hilgersmarket.com

Hilger's Friendly Market starts the year with morels and asparagus in April and keeps the goods coming all the way through October, when the pumpkins are ready to be picked. The associated farm gets especially busy during its Fall Pumpkin Festival, with food, contests, games, hayrides, and all sorts of fun for the whole family. At this time of year Hilger's receives a steady stream of yellow busses as schoolkids show up for group field trips. For many families in the region and beyond, a fall visit to Hilger's is a favorite tradition. Others are year-round customers, stopping by weekly during the growing season for fresh fruits and vegetables. Hilger's Friendly Market is open year-round and seven days a week—Sundays from 11:00 AM to 6:00 PM and Mondays through Saturdays from 9:00 AM to 7:00 PM.

Kercher's Sunrise Orchards

APPLES, APPLE PRODUCTS, MUSHROOMS

> 19498 CR 38, Goshen IN 46526 (Elkhart)
> www.kerchersorchard.com

The Kercher family has operated their orchard since

1922. Their 13 varieties of apples are available in their on-farm market, or visitors can pick their own. The market also offers their popular October Gold Cider. In April of each year, Kercher's is the regional destination for morel mushrooms. To help celebrate morels, Kercher's holds a contest for the biggest one that can be found. The winner gets a cash prize of $25, a cement morel lawn ornament, and braggin' rights for a whole year. Fall tours of the orchard are popular with people of all ages. One special feature of the tour is a 20-minute film tracing the apple from blossom to market. Kercher's is open year-round, Mondays through Fridays from 8:30 AM to 5:30 PM and Saturdays from 8:30 AM to 5:00 PM. In May, September, and October it is also open Sundays from 12 noon to 5:00 PM.

Little Crow Foods

BAKING AND COATING MIXES, BREAKFAST CEREALS

201 S. Detroit St., Warsaw IN 46581 (Kosciusko)
800-288-2769 • www.littlecrowfoods.com

Several generations have breakfast-table memories of warm bowls of chocolaty CoCo Wheats. Little Crow Foods' signature product appeared in 1930, but the company has existed since 1903, when it was founded as a flour mill. Soon it began offering foods that have become familiar household names. In the years since the launch of CoCo Wheats, Little Crow has introduced Fryin' Magic and Bakin' Miracle coating mixes, Miracle Maize cornbread and muffin mix, and FastShake pancake mix. These products can be found in most grocery stores and can also be ordered online.

Orchard Hill Farms

APPLES, APPLE PRODUCTS

11061 E. 415 N., Kendallville IN 46755 (Noble)
260-347-3682 • www.orchardhillfarms.com

Orchard Hill Farms grows 14 different kinds of apples. It also makes its own all-natural cider, apple butter, apple jelly, and apple syrup. All of these items can be purchased at the farm retail store. Apples are also available in bulk, from three-pound bags to bushels. The store is open Mondays through Saturdays from 8:00 AM to 6:00 PM and Sundays from 1:00 to 5:00 PM, except that from November 1 to February 1 hours are reduced to 9:00 AM to 5:00 PM Mondays though Saturdays. Tours of the packing facility and cider operation are also available and include a wagon ride through the orchard as well. Call to schedule one.

Pathway Pastures

BEEF, LAMB, CHICKEN, TURKEY, PORK

6037 CR 52, St. Joe IN 46785 (DeKalb)
260-337-0101 • www.pathwaypastures.com

Pathway Pastures can satisfy the taste buds of nearly every conscientious carnivore. The farm raises cattle, lambs, chickens, pigs, and Thanksgiving turkeys, all without hormones or antibiotics. The animals get to live on the pasture and do what animals like to do. For beef, Pathway Pastures settled on the Ruby Red Devon breed. Rare in the U.S. today, Devon cattle were brought over by the Pilgrims on the Mayflower and raised by George Washington at his Mount Vernon farm. Devons were selected for a number of reasons, including their exceptional taste. For information about how to order Pathway Pastures' products, call or visit the website.

Northeast Indiana

Sechler's Pickles

PICKLES

5686 SR 1, St. Joe IN 46785 (DeKalb)
260-337-5461 • www.gourmetpickles.com

Ralph Sechler got his start in the pickle business in 1914, and the Sechler family still operates the business. Their first product was Genuine Dill Pickles, which are still available today as Genuine "Aged in Wood" Dill Pickles. Sweet relish and sweet pickles soon followed, including Candied Sweet Orange Strip Pickles and Pasteurized "Fresh Pack" pickles; today Sechler's has 45 items in its product line. To make its pickles, Sechler's gets freshly picked cucumbers from farmers across northern Indiana, northwest Ohio, and southern Michigan. Its products can be found in many grocery stores and also ordered online. Sechler's welcomes group tours. Check the website for details.

Seven Sons Meat Company

BEEF, PORK, CHICKEN

15718 Aboite Rd., Roanoke IN 46783 (Huntington)
877-620-1977 • www.sevensons.net

The Seven Sons Meat Company is a big family business. It's not necessarily the business that is big, though, it's the family—Lee Hitzfield, his wife Beth, and their seven sons and *their* families. At one time the Hitzfields ran a conventional hog farm, but a series of both personal and professional circumstances prompted them to transition to an "intensive grazing operation," raising entirely grass-fed beef, free-range pork, and pastured chicken. Their products are available at their farm store, and their beef can also be found at several retail locations around the state or ordered online. The farm store is open daily from 8:00 AM to 8:00 PM.

Swissland Cheese Company

CHEESE

818 Welty St., Berne IN 46711 (Adams)
260-589-2761 • www.swisslandcheese.com

Swissland Cheese makes raw milk, grass-fed organic, and specialty cheeses from goat and cow milk. Much of its milk comes from the Old Order Amish community near Berne. Swissland is Indiana's only producer of goat milk feta. The company also has a line of specialty cheeses, most of which start with Cheddar as a base. These include Chedda Choco Nut, a sweet and salty combination of Cheddar, cocoa, and English walnuts, and Chedda Feta Bluz, a mixture of Cheddar, feta, and blue cheeses. Its products are available online and at Swissland's Cheese Outlet (818 Welty St.) in Berne. Store hours are Mondays through Fridays from 9:00 AM to 5:00 PM and Saturdays from 8:00 AM to 1:00 PM.

Yoder's Meat & Cheese Company

MEATS AND CHEESES

435 S. Van Buren St., Shipshewana IN 46565 (LaGrange)
260-768-4715 • www.yodersmeatshoppe.com

Yoder's is a full-service, family-owned butcher shop offering more than 100 cuts of beef, pork, lamb, and chicken, as well as a full line of smoked meats, with more than 17 varieties of jerky. All the meat comes from animals raised by the Yoder family or by other nearby farmers. The Yoders use animals that are fed only grain and hay

Northeast Indiana

with no additives, fillers, or chemicals. As for cheese, Yoder's carries more than 75 varieties, most of them made by Amish and Mennonite cheese makers in Indiana and nearby in Ohio. The shop is open from 8:00 AM to 5:00 PM Mondays through Saturdays, and many products can be ordered online.

MAKE EATING LOCAL A YEAR-ROUND FAMILY AFFAIR

Hoosiers are busy people. When it comes to eating, speed and convenience seem like necessities, especially for families with young kids. The grocery store down the street is going to be where most of us get the large majority of our food. We're fortunate to have such an affordable and accessible supply. Unless we tell them differently, the kids in our lives are likely to think that all food comes in cardboard boxes or wrapped in plastic, or is handed to us through drive-through windows.

Educators tell us there are "teachable moments" in children's lives. Every meal can be an opportunity to teach kids healthy eating habits that can last a lifetime. Having a hard time getting a three-year-old to eat carrots? Plant some in your backyard and let her dig them out of the ground. She just might be more inclined to have a taste. Use this book to plan some family experiences to get kids closer to the source of their food. Here we offer a plan for a different Indiana food experience each month of the year. So shop at the local mega-mart during the week if you need to, but reserve a few hours of weekend time for some of these excursions and experiences.

- January—Pick up pork or beef at a winter farmers' market and ask the farmer what life for a pig and a cow is like at his farm.

- February—Visit a dairy and watch the cows get milked. Pick up a farmstead cheese and use it for grilled cheese sandwiches on a cold Saturday afternoon.

- March—Take in one of Indiana's many maple syrup festivals and eat pancakes—lots and lots of pancakes.

- April—Hunt for morels, pick up some local fresh asparagus, and roast a locally raised leg of lamb for Passover or Easter.

- May—Be first in line on the opening day of the summer farmers' market.

- June—Get local strawberries and invite the neighbors over to eat shortcake on the front porch.

- July—Have a tomato day, using Indiana tomatoes in all three meals—fold them into an omelet, stack them onto your BLT, and slice them into your dinner salad.

- August—Beat the heat with a chilled Indiana watermelon. Invite the neighbors over again.

- September—Visit a U-Pick apple orchard, then go home and bake a pie while sipping cider.

- October—Get your Halloween pumpkin from a pumpkin farm instead of from in front of the suburban big-box store.

- November—Get a locally raised turkey and, when giving thanks at the dinner table, remember the farm family who raised it.

- December—Have a Charles Dickens holiday dinner! Get a locally raised goose for the holidays and talk with a British accent throughout the meal.

EATING LOCAL WHILE DINING OUT

Amish Acres Restaurant Barn
1600 W. Market St., Nappanee IN 46550 (Elkhart)
800-800-4942 • www.amishacres.com
See p. 58

Blue Gate Restaurant
105 E. Middlebury St., Shipshewana IN 46565 (LaGrange)
260-768-4725 • www.riegsecker.com
See p. 59

Blue Gill Restaurant
133 S. Main St., Goshen IN 46526 (Elkhart)
574-534-4000 • www.thebluegill.net

Indigo on 17
56039 Parkway Ave., Elkhart IN 46516 (Elkhart)
574-293-1717 • www.indigoon17.com
See p. 47

Joseph Decuis Restaurant and Heritage Farm
191 N. Main St., Roanoke IN 46783 (Huntington)
260-672-1715 • www.josephdecuis.com
See p. 50

Lucchese's
655 CR 17, Elkhart IN 46516 (Elkhart)
574-522-4137

FARMERS' MARKETS

Allen County Ag Produce Association Farmers' Market
3300 Warsaw St., Fort Wayne IN 46807 (Allen)
April to November, Wednesdays 8:00 AM to 4:00 PM,
    Saturdays 7:00 AM to 1:00 PM

American Countryside Farmers' Market
27751 CR 26, Elkhart IN 46517 (Elkhart)
Open year-round, Hours change seasonally—check website
www.americancountryside.us

Fulton County Farmers' Market
815 N. Main St., Rochester IN 46975 (Fulton)
May–October, Wednesdays 3:00 to 7:00 PM,
    Saturdays 7:30 AM to 12 noon

Goshen Farmers' Market
212 W. Washington St., Goshen IN 46526 (Elkhart)
Open year-round, Tuesdays 3:00 to 7:00 PM (May–October),
    Saturdays 8:00 AM to 1:00 PM (year-round)
www.millrace.org

North Manchester Farmers' Market
Intersection of Main and Walnut Streets
North Manchester IN 46962 (Wabash)
June–October, Saturdays 8:00 AM to 12 noon

Northeast Indiana

WINERIES

Satek Winery
6208 N. Van Guilder Rd., Fremont IN 46737 (Steuben)
260-495-WINE (9463) • www.satekwinery.com

MICROBREWERIES & BREWPUBS

Mad Anthony Brewing
2002 Broadway Ave., Fort Wayne IN 46802 (Allen)
260-426-2537 • www.madbrew.com

Warbird Brewing Company
10515 Majic Port Lane, Fort Wayne IN 46814 (Allen)
260-459-2400 • www.warbirdbrewing.com

FOOD FESTIVALS

74

Home Grown Indiana

Cornfest
Indiana sweet corn and corn-inspired fun
Huntington IN (Huntington)
Mid-August
260-356-9681

Ligonier's Marshmallow Festival
*Marshmallow roast, marshmallow games,
    and a marshmallow bake-off*
Ligonier IN (Noble)
Late August/Early September
260-341-0707 • www.themarshmallowfestival.com

Nappanee Apple Festival
Apple baking, peeling, and pie-eating contests and apple goodies
Nappanee IN 46550 (Elkhart)
Mid-September
574-773-7812 • www.nappaneeapplefestival.org

St. Joe Pickle Festival
Fried pickles, pickle ice cream, and a pickle-decorating contest
St. Joe IN (DeKalb)
2nd week of August
260-337-5470 • www.sechlerspickles.com

Very Berry Strawberry Festival
Wabash IN (Wabash)
A variety of strawberry treats
Early June
260-563-0975 • www.wabashmarketplace.org

Wakarusa Maple Syrup Festival
Pancakes and baking contest
Wakarusa IN (Elkhart)
Late April
574-862-4344 • www.wakarusamaplesyrupfestival.com

3

Home Grown Indiana

NORTH CENTRAL

White

Cass

Miami

Benton

Carroll

Howard

Grant

Blackford

Jay

Warren

Tippecanoe

Clinton

Tipton

Fountain

Madison

Delaware

Randolph

Vermillion

Montgomery

Henry

Wayne

Parke

Putnam

North Central

We've been a tad bit inclusive with our definition of "north central Indiana." This chapter takes a look at a large region north of the Indianapolis metro area and south of northwest and northeast Indiana, stretching across to the Illinois border on the west and the Ohio border on the east. The three largest cities in this area are Lafayette/West Lafayette, Kokomo, and Muncie. The communities surrounding the two large universities, Purdue and Ball State, have a food scene typical of college towns—fast, cheap, and open late. There are lots of eating-out options in that category. Thanks to Purdue's many international students, West Lafayette has terrific locally owned ethnic eateries. Kokomo, with its hungry manufacturing workforce laboring around the clock, has developed an interesting food culture as well, with lots of hearty home-style cooking, Louie's Coney Island's famous "bakes," and Lord-Jon's Tacos. Kokomo is also home to Indiana's first 24-hour Starbucks.

When it comes to locally grown and produced food, north central Indiana has much to offer, with a number of farmers and growers and a short but impressive list of restaurants serving local foods. Standouts in the region include one of the nation's largest tomato processors—Red Gold in Elwood uses acres and acres of Indiana tomatoes to keep grocery stores and pantries across the country stocked with their tomato products. Humphrey Family Farms in Williamsport raises all sorts of birds—turkeys, ducks, geese, and chickens. The region is also home to the state's only meadery, New Day, which makes several versions of what may be the world's oldest adult beverage.

Cooley Family Farm

PRODUCE

24 N. 900 E., Lafayette IN 47905 (Tippecanoe)
765-296-8834 • www.cooleyfamilyfarm.com

Kevin, Tracy, and little Trae Michael are the "family" on the Cooley Family Farm, and they've built a solid reputation for offering perhaps the widest variety of produce in north central Indiana. They have 20 acres in production, on which they grow hundreds of varieties of fruits and vegetables, many of them open-pollinated or heirloom varieties, all grown without synthetic insecticides, herbicides, or fertilizers.

The Cooleys start their season with spring lettuce, radishes, bunching onions, arugula, spinach, turnips, peas, rhubarb, and strawberries. As the season progresses they add beans, beets, kohlrabi, potatoes, and tomatoes. Following closely behind are sweet corn, cucumbers, pickles, summer squash, onions, okra, herbs, flowers, zucchini, and peppers. Later in the season they add winter squash, pumpkins, gourds, corn shocks, and melons.

Several spring crops are grown again in the winter with the aid of high tunnels. These are plastic-covered structures resembling greenhouses but without permanent heating, cooling, or lighting systems. Plants are grown directly in the soil inside the tunnels and ventilation is provided by opening doors or windows or rolling up the sides. The Cooleys' regular market season runs from early May to the end of October, but with the tunnels, they can extend the season. The produce grown over the winter is available to a select group of customers via an email distribution list.

The Cooleys' farm is visible along SR 26 at 900 E. Customers who pass the farm daily get to see the fields come to life as the Cooleys plant, nurture, and harvest their crops. In a testament to their all-natural farming practices, it is also common to see them enjoying a fresh-from-the-ground snack as they work.

The Cooleys sell their produce at the Sagamore West Farmers' Market and the Downtown Lafayette Farmers' Market. Customers can also enjoy shopping on the farm, using the Cooleys' self-serve honor system. Customers simply select the products they want at the farm stand, list them on a ticket, and place the ticket and payment in a payment slot. They can even email requests a day in advance; if their choices are available, they receive an email confirmation and their order is waiting when they arrive.

The Cooleys also offer a what they call a Harvest Basket service, which is similar to a CSA. In return for a lump-sum payment at the beginning of the season, subscribers receive a weekly basket full of Cooley's fruits and vegetables. Demand for the baskets is high, so subscriptions are limited. Harvest Basket subscribers are also invited to an annual gathering and farm tour to learn more about where their food is coming from.

Adding together basket subscribers, farmers' market customers, and visitors to the farm stand, we can see that a significant number of north central Indiana families are enjoying some of the freshest fruits and vegetables in the region.

The Juniper Spoon Catering Kitchen

CATERER

100 W. Main St., Darlington IN 47940 (Montgomery)
765-794-0533 • www.thejuniperspoon.com

Imagine sitting down at the dinner table with your family for a meal that includes seasonal fruits and vegetables from the garden, beef or pork from a nearby farm where you know the farmer treated his animals well and didn't load them up with growth hormones or antibiotics, and a heavenly crème brûlée for dessert made from eggs gathered that very morning from the henhouse. For most of us this is some sort of Martha Stewart–meets–Laura Ingalls Wilder fantasy. But for a growing number of families in Montgomery County it's a reality. The real kicker is that they don't have to lift one finger to enjoy such a feast. These are people who purchase home-delivered meals from The Juniper Spoon. Guests at wedding receptions, attendees at corporate functions, and other groups throughout central Indiana are also benefiting from the fruits (and vegetables) of The Juniper Spoon's labor.

The Juniper Spoon is the family business of chef (and former organic farmer) Lali Hess and her husband Doug Miller, an organic gardener and full-time student. The Hess/Miller enterprise is a unique whole-foods catering service creating fresh and inspired dishes for large and small events as well as family dinners. Lali and Doug describe their food as hand-crafted, and they use original recipes influenced by traditional dishes. For ingredients, they turn to their own organic garden and year-round greenhouse, and the family farms that surround them. Their commitment to fresh and local foods is rooted in their commitment to strengthening the local economy, supporting the bio-region, and serving food that just plain tastes better.

Their full-service catering operation can do it all, from hors d'oeuvres and "conversation platters" to lunches and dinners. Their culinary repertoire includes vegetarian options and a United Nations' worth of ethnic dishes—African, Asian, Eastern European, Indian, Latin American, Middle Eastern, and Spanish. All dishes are made from scratch and rely on whole foods rather than overprocessed short cuts.

Currently they deliver dinners only in the Crawfordsville and Montgomery County area, but growing demand from other parts of central Indiana could prompt them to expand. For the catering side of the business, Hess and company offer a choice of services—buffets for large events and seated meals for smaller affairs. One look at the catering menu confirms that there is a lot of creativity at work—the brunch menu offers Homemade Granola with Organic Yogurt and Fruit, the lunch menu suggests Butternut Squash Soup with Apples and Sage, dinner could include Almond-Encrusted Salmon with Lemon Leek Sauce and Rice Pilaf, and a conversation platter of Indiana Artisan Cheeses is always tasty.

We've all had ninety-nine unimaginatively catered meals for every one that was creative and memorable. Cold-cut platters and chafing dishes of dried-out, flavorless lasagna seem to be the norm. After learning about The Juniper Spoon we might take desperate measures to get into one of their events—crash a wedding reception or a ladies' tea, or maybe even change jobs to get in on one of Hess's corporate gigs.

EQUINOX RELISH

Lali Hess makes this tasty relish each year around the third weekend of September. It is a great way to use an enormous quantity of banana peppers, hot wax peppers, or hot peppers. This is absolutely delicious on pizza, crusty bread, sandwiches, eggs, rice and beans, pork chops, and lots, lots more. This recipe makes four quarts or eight pints of relish.

- 1 peck (about a paper grocery bag full) banana peppers (yellow, orange, or red stage) hot wax peppers, or combination of peppers
- 6 stalks celery, chopped
- 1 quart apple cider vinegar
- 3 cups water
- 2 cups canola oil or combination of canola and olive (do not use all olive oil)
- 3–6 cloves garlic, minced
- ¼ cup dried oregano or the leaves from 5 large sprigs of fresh oregano
- ¾ cup salt

Wash the peppers and cut into rings, removing most of the seeds and the stems. Stuff them into glass gallon jars.

In a large pitcher, thoroughly mix the remaining ingredients. Pour this brine over the peppers to fill the jars to the top. Cover and allow to sit at room temperature overnight or up to 3 days, shaking the jars up a bit a few times each day.

Transfer the peppers and their brine to glass quart or pint canning jars and fit with rings and lids. Do not process them. Kept refrigerated, the peppers will last about 6 months. You can continue to add fresh pepper rings to the brine until the first frost.

Maize: An American Grill

RESTAURANT

112 N. 3rd St., Lafayette IN 47901 (Tippecanoe)
765-429-6125 • www.maizeinc.com

When co-owners Christie and Brannon Soileau set up shop in Lafayette, their vision was to offer traditional American cuisine with an international eclectic flair.

Maize is a place where Midwesterners can find the non-threatening foods they are accustomed to, but with an unexpected twist. For instance, catfish is expected, but Chili Lime Aioli Dipping Sauce—that's an unexpected twist. This is the formula at Maize. Pastas, chops, fish, and other standard fare are all served with something special from the mind of Brannon Soileau.

The development of a chef usually begins in childhood, and this was true of Brannon. With his football-coach dad on the road much of the time, young Brannon spent lots of time with his mom in her southern Louisiana kitchen, watching her create gumbos, pot roasts, and fried chicken. As he searched for his own place in life, he ended up back in the kitchen, first as a student at the Culinary Institute of America, where he met Christie, and later at some great restaurants in several towns. He eventually landed the job of executive chef at the 480-seat Pump Room in Chicago.

After several years of working for others, Brannon and Christie settled in Lafayette to begin their own venture. From the beginning, Brannon insisted on the highest-quality ingredients, whether from near or far. They import seafood from Seattle, pumpkin seed oil from southern Germany, and many fresh ingredients from just a couple blocks or a few miles away. To create their menu, Chef Soileau draws on some of the best Indiana home-grown foods—farm-raised duck, Amish chicken, Indiana lamb that rivals Colorado's best, and in-season heirloom tomatoes and other vegetables from a local master gardener. Maize is open from 5:30 to 9:00 PM Mondays through Thursdays and from 5:30 to 11:00 PM Fridays and Saturdays. Reservations are recommended.

North Central Indiana

SHAGBARK CHEESECAKE

This cheesecake from Chef Brannon Soileau's kitchen is flavored with Shagbark Hickory Syrup from Hickoryworks in Trafalgar (see p. 116). Use farm-fresh eggs to make it especially rich and delicious.

Crust

- ½ cup pecans, toasted and chopped
- ½ cup graham cracker crumbs
- 1 tablespoon brown sugar
- 1 teaspoon cocoa powder
- ¼ cup (½ stick) butter, melted

Filling

- 2 pounds cream cheese, room temperature
- ½ teaspoon powdered ginger
- ¼ teaspoon salt
- 6 eggs, room temperature
- 1⅓ cups Shagbark Hickory Syrup, room temperature

Preheat oven to 350°. In a medium bowl, combine all the crust ingredients. Press into a buttered 10" springform pan. Bake crust for 10 minutes. Leave the oven on after removing the crust.

Using a mixer, cream together the cream cheese, ginger, and salt, scraping bowl frequently. Add the eggs and then the syrup, creaming each thoroughly and scraping the bowl as needed. Pour into the crust, and tightly wrap the bottom and sides of pan with foil. Set pan in a hot water bath (see below) and place in the oven.

Bake until the top of the cheesecake is lightly browned, but the center still jiggles slightly, about 45 minutes. Cool the cake in the pan on a rack. Cover with plastic wrap and refrigerate overnight before serving. To remove the cake from *the pan, run a knife around the edges to release them from the pan. Release the springform pan and remove the ring.*

To make a water bath, put the filled springform pan in a larger pan and add enough boiling water to reach halfway up the side of the springform pan.

New Day Meadery

HONEY WINE

> 701 S. Anderson St., Elwood IN 46036 (Madison)
> 765-552-3433 • www.newdaymeadery.com

People-watchers know that it's fun to speculate about passing strangers—their jobs, their relationships, the intimate details of their lives. Someone who saw Brett Canaday and Tia Agnew at a trendy club in Indy might think them young ad executives, or up-and-coming corporate attorneys. "Practitioners of the ancient art of mead making" would be way, way down on the list of their possible occupations.

But that's exactly what Canaday and Agnew are. They are the proprietors of New Day Meadery in Elwood. The journey that took them into the world of mead may be atypical, but it is logical. A Purdue University food science degree, a bee-keeping hobby, an appreciation for all things fermented, a passion for local foods, and the desire to start a business all converged in their lives. What began as a hobby for themselves and friends quickly became the business they were looking for and New Day Meadery was born. It is the only meadery in Indiana and one of only about 50 in the U.S.

If the only thing you know about mead is what you remember reading in *Beowulf*, here is a little primer. Mead is simply a wine made from honey, and it is probably the oldest alcoholic beverage. Just like wine from grapes, mead can be made dry or sweet, still or sparkling, and with a range of alcoholic content. While a few Indiana wineries grow some of their own grapes, most get them from somewhere else in the world and then make wine here. In contrast, New Day's half-dozen varieties of mead are 100 percent local, made with both local fruits and local honeys. New Day makes two traditional meads, a dry and a semi-dry. The dry mead can be compared to sake, but without the high-alcohol punch. It pairs beautifully with Asian flavors like light soy and ginger. The semi-dry has a slight sweetness to it and works with fruit and cheese as well as Thai and Indian dishes. Three fruit varieties are also available—peach, blueberry, and red raspberry.

New Day's Elwood facility includes a tasting room that is open May through November on Fridays, Saturdays, and Sundays. Private group tastings can be arranged by appointment. Tastings at New Day are as educational as they are delicious. Canaday and Agnew's passion for and dedication to wine making and local foods are infectious. Their mead costs between $16 and $24 per bottle, with a 10 percent discount for purchase of a case (including mixed cases). They also sell at many of central Indiana's markets. Their website has detailed information about where to locate New Day's fine meads.

Shoup's Country Foods

PORK

2048 South SR 39, Frankfort IN 46041 (Clinton)
800-MINI-HOG (800-646-4464)
www.shoupscountry.com

Shoup's Country Foods is an Indiana institution. It

started as a small custom plant, processing Indiana pork. As its popularity grew, Shoup's opened a nationwide mail-order operation as well as a retail store, and Shoup's meats are available in grocery stores in Indiana and surrounding states. Catering is also available.

This family business is run by Tom and Carol Shoup and their three daughters—Cindy, Amy, and Cheri. The family takes care of all aspects of the business, and after a full week of working together, still manages to get together for a big Sunday dinner. The day consists of good food and lots of rest and play, including fishing on their pond and pony rides for the grandkids.

Shoup's has three main pork products—the Mini-Hog Roast, Porkburgers, and Pulled Pork Barbecue. The cornerstone of the business is the Mini-Hog Roast, a boneless pork roast which comes seasoned and ready to cook on the grill or in the oven. The roast is available in two sizes. The five-pound family size will feed 10–12 people, and the 12-pound party size will feed a hungry crowd of 20–25. Shoup's Porkburgers are a regular feature at many central and north central Indiana fairs and festivals. A great alternative to beef burgers, these patties are 90 percent lean and made from 100 percent pure ground pork. Each retail pack includes 20 ¼ lb. porkburgers. And the Pulled Pork Barbecue is made from lean pork, pulled and smothered with Shoup's own barbecue sauce. It comes in 1-pound packages.

The perfect accompaniments to any of these are Shoup's Seasoning or Barbecue Sauce. The sauce is zesty and brown-sugar sweet. The seasoning is a special blend of spices that has been in the family for more than 30 years. It was created to accompany their pork but works equally well on beef and poultry. And tasty as the seasoning and sauce are on their own, the combination is even better. They were named "Indiana's Best" at a recent

World Pork Expo. Both the sauce and the seasoning can be found in many Indiana grocery stores, often in the meat department.

Shoup's also offers full-service catering and can accommodate both casual and more formal affairs. The pork products are popular, but many other selections are available as well. More information about catering is available on the website.

Shoup's products can be ordered online and also purchased at a retail location in Frankfort. The store carries an even wider variety of meats, including steaks and beef burgers. All cuts are available individually or in quantities that can fill up your freezer. The store is open Tuesdays through Fridays from 8:00 AM to 5:00 PM and Saturdays from 8:00 AM to 12 noon. It is closed on Sundays and Mondays.

Two Cookin' Sisters Specialty Food Co. and the Prairie Street Market

SALSA AND RETAIL SHOP

210 S. Prairie St., Brookston IN 47923 (White)
765-563-7377 • www.bigsistersalsa.com

Kim Robinson and Kristi Robinson Rensberger (a.k.a. Two Cookin' Sisters) just might be a pair of DNA-sharing evil geniuses. Beneath their Brookston shop there is probably a secret test-kitchen lair where they concoct their diabolically delicious products. Once having consumed these salsas, jams, jellies, and other delights, the masses become hopelessly addicted and can't go more than a few long weeks between fixes.

The sisters' first product was "Big Sister Salsa," which remains their signature item and carries the eye-catching tag line "It's Loud and Bossy." Younger siblings of loud and bossy big sisters might buy it for the name alone. The pleasantly surprising taste, however, will be what makes them regular customers. Peppers are first on its list of ingredients, which means that peppers are the predominant ingredient. Nearly every other salsa lists tomatoes first. But tomatoes are number two in Big Sister Salsa; and with peppers in the lead role, it tastes very different from most other salsas. Sweet and spicy peppers commingle to deliver a complex blast to the palate. Loud and bossy? Yes, but in an endearing way, much like some older sisters.

One of the sisters' more recently introduced products is Carrot Cake Jam. Like all Two Cookin' Sisters' products, it bears an impressively simple list of ingredients. Here is the full inventory of a jar of Carrot Cake Jam: sugar, carrots, pears, pineapple, lemon juice, cinnamon, nutmeg, cloves, and pectin. That's it. Michael Pollan, author of *The Omnivore's Dilemma,* says that we should try to eat foods that pass the "great-grandmother test"—foods our great-grandmothers would recognize as food. This would certainly pass.

Another thing to love about this product is the Ball jar it comes in. A sort of gentle nostalgic breeze blows each time a Ball jar is opened for the first time—unscrewing the outer ring, reaching for a knife to gently pry up the metal disk that tops the jar, that little pop, and then the unfettered goodness inside. Opening up a jar of Carrot Cake Jam confirms that it really does taste like carrot cake—fruity, with a bit of carrot crunch, and infused with warm spices. It is delicious on lightly buttered toast and it is even better on a bagel with cream cheese.

In 2006, the sisters took over the space adjacent to their Brookston storefront. At their Prairie Street Market you can find local, in-season produce, eggs, cheese, and plenty of other good stuff. The combination of the original shop and the new market are definitely worth the trip to Brookston, just a few miles north of Lafayette. Both shops are open Tuesdays through Saturdays from 10:00 AM to 6:00 PM. And between trips, if you simply can't make it there, you can stock up on Two Cookin' Sisters products by ordering from their website.

Aubrey's Meats

BEEF, PORK

> 8570 N. 750 W., Elwood IN 46036 (Madison)
> 765-552-0922 • www.aubreysnaturalmeats.com

Aubrey's Natural Meats' claim to fame is that it is the Midwest's only custom cutter and packager of all-natural meats. All of Sarah and Cary Aubrey's beef and pork comes from Indiana farmers who do not use hormones, steroids, or antibiotics on their animals. They will process and deliver your beef or pork nearly any way you can imagine. Their list of available cuts includes some of the harder-to-find cuts like beef shank, flat iron steak, and oxtails. The Aubreys dry-age their beef for at least two weeks before trimming it, and their pork for five to seven days. They provide home delivery in the Indianapolis metro area, and they also sell at the Noblesville and Fishers Farmers' Markets.

Brown Family Farm

BEEF, LAMB, EGGS

> 8983 East SR 18, Montpelier IN 47359 (Blackford)
> 765-728-2133 • www.brownfamilyfarm.com

The Browns have been farming this land in Blackford County since 1852. Their focus these days is on providing drug-free, grass-fed beef and lamb and pastured eggs.

Farmer Craig Brown is working on a commercial kitchen to take his prepared foods public, selling brats, burgers, breakfast burritos, and more at area farmers' markets. Visitors are welcome at the farm (call first!). Check the web site or call for details of market sales.

Butera Family Orchard

FRUIT

> 1443 W. 800 S., Lafayette IN 47909 (Tippecanoe)
> 765-538-3373

The harvest at Butera Family Orchard begins in May with strawberries and progresses with sour cherries, blackberries, peaches, nectarines, and pears. Apples, the orchard's mainstay, are available from early July, when the Lodis are ready for picking, through mid-October, which brings the Granny Smiths. In between, an additional 13 varieties come to harvest. The orchard has been in operation since 1983; former city dwellers Joe and Carolyn Butera purchased it in 2005. During the season, their fruit is available at the orchard Monday through Saturday. When they have extra produce, they can also be found at the Lafayette Farmers' Market.

English's Buffalo Farm

BISON

> 6432 North US 231, Bainbridge IN 46105 (Putnam)
> 765-522-7777 • www.englishsbuffalofarm.com

John and Sheila English have been operating their Bainbridge farm since 1997 and their buffalo herd now numbers more than 80. Visitors have about a 50/50 chance of seeing the animals, since buffalo tend to stay together

North Central Indiana

and sometimes are not roaming where they can be seen. The Englishes sell the meat at their on-farm Trading Post and also ship it. Cuts include steaks, roasts, stewing meat, ground bison, and summer sausage. The Trading Post also sells Native American books, crafts, and much more. It is open year-round, Fridays, Saturdays, and Sundays from 12 noon until 5:00 PM.

Grabow Orchard and Bakery

APPLES, BAKED GOODS, PRODUCE

> 6397 SR 13, Pendleton IN 46064 (Madison)
> 888-534-3225 • www.graboworchard.com

When Grabow Orchard and Bakery opened in the early 1990s, lots of Hoosiers adopted a new tradition of family visits to the orchard. Fall is an especially popular time to visit, with attractions including 20 different kinds of apples, a pumpkin patch, a bakery, and an annual apple dumpling festival. In 2001, a crew from the Food Network showed up and Grabow's Apple Dumplings became an overnight national sensation. They are now shipped all over the U.S. Fortunately, fame did not go to the Grabows' heads, and they continue to offer the same friendly service and festive environment they always have. Hours vary throughout the year, so check the website first for information on hours and events.

Hoosier Grassfed Beef

BEEF

> 3959 North SR 341, Attica IN 47918 (Fountain)
> 765-538-2888 • www.hoosiergrassfedbeef.com

Hoosier Grassfed Beef is a family-owned farm. The DeSutter and Hollinger families established it in 2000 with the goal of working in concert with nature to produce healthy and delicious beef. They have succeeded in that mission and have developed a reputation as a leader in conservation practices. Their cattle are raised on fresh green pasture and are never fed grain. (See "Why Grass-fed Beef?" on p. 251.) Their beef contains no artificial preservatives or growth hormones. Beef is available year-round and is sold only in bulk—quarters, halves, and wholes. Orders are taken by phone and email.

Humphrey Family Farm

POULTRY

> 3981 S. Grant St., Williamsport IN 47993 (Warren)
> 765-762-3160

For some reason, the tradition of the Christmas goose did not make it across the pond in any significant way. If you are interested in bringing a Dickensian flavor to your holiday plans, Humphrey Family Farm in Williamsport offers all-natural geese and several other kinds of birds, including heritage turkeys. Call the Humphreys to reserve birds, which can be picked up at the farm. The Humphreys also take holiday orders at Trader's Point Creamery in Zionsville in the weeks leading up to Thanksgiving and Christmas. Arrangements can be made to pick up birds there as well. In the words of Tiny Tim, "God bless us, every one."

Meadow Valley Farm

CHEESE

> 4102 N. 400 E., Rockville IN 47872 (Parke)
> 765-597-2306

Samuel Stoltzfus has been a cheese maker since 2000 and his raw milk cheeses can be found on the menu of Chef Rick Bayless's famous Frontera Grill in Chicago (www.rickbayless.com). Meadow Valley makes eight different raw milk cheeses—Cheddar, Colby, Monterey Jack, Havarti, Gouda, Baby Swiss, Jalapeño, and Pepper Jack. All are made with milk from the farm's Jersey cows. Meadow Valley Farms cheeses are available at several natural foods markets across the state and beyond, and also at the shop on the farm, open Mondays through Fridays from 7:00 AM to 5:00 PM and Saturdays from 7:00 AM to 4:00 PM.

Minnetrista Orchard Shop

RETAIL SHOP

> 311 W. Saint Joseph St., Muncie IN 47303 (Delaware)
> 765-282-4848

When a weekend trip to the farmers' market doesn't fit into the schedule, fresh produce, eggs, meat, goat cheese, and handmade salsa can be picked up during the week at the Minnetrista Orchard Shop. The shop also features specialty foods, kitchen items and baking aids, fresh apples and cider in season, and made-to-order gift baskets for all occasions. The store is open Mondays through Saturdays from 8:00 AM to 4:00 PM and Saturdays from 11:00 AM to 4:00 PM.

Mr. Happy Burger

RESTAURANT

> West Location
> 900 W. Market St., Logansport IN 46947 (Cass)
> 574-753-4016
>
> East Location
> 3131 E. Market St., Logansport IN 46947 (Cass)
> 574-753-6418

Bob Shanks is no johnny-come-lately when it comes to serving local foods. It wasn't some marketing study that prompted him to use local beef for his burgers, and it wasn't *Time*'s 2007 cover article asking "Is Local the New Organic?" that prompted him to serve brats made from locally grown and processed pork. Nope, it just made good business sense to him to use what was available right there in Cass County. That was his thought in the early 1960s when he opened the first Mr. Happy Burger, and that is why he has kept up the practice for more than 45 years. Both Mr. Happy Burger locations are open Mondays through Saturdays from 10:45 AM. The westside location closes at 9:00 PM every night, and the eastside location closes at 10:00 PM Mondays through Thursdays and at 11:00PM Fridays and Saturdays.

My Dad's Sweet Corn

SWEET CORN

> 2579 S. 500 W., Tipton IN 46072 (Tipton)
> 765-675-4519 • www.mydadssweetcorn.com

Allen Baird, of My Dad's Sweet Corn, specializes in selling just one thing—sweet corn. He's been farming commercial corn and soybeans since the '60s, but even then he always planted a few rows of sweet corn. His son convinced him to share his delicious sweet corn with more than just the family, so Allen started planting a few acres of it instead of a few rows. When you make a purchase you can be assured that your ears of corn were on the stalk less than 24 hours earlier. During the week, you can buy his corn at Joe's Butcher Shop in Carmel, on Wednesdays at the Indianapolis City Market's Farmers' Market, on Thursday afternoons at the Abundant Life Church Farmers' Market in Indianapolis, and on the weekends at the Fishers, Noblesville, Carmel, and Binford farmers' markets. He will also deliver orders of more than ten dozen ears to Indianapolis and northside locations.

Prairie Moon Orchard and Market

APPLES, PRODUCE, BAKED GOODS

PO Box 627, Monon IN 47959 (White)
219-253-6383 • www.prairiemoonorchard.com

Prairie Moon has more than 13 lush acres of apple orchards growing 18 varieties of apples. Jim and Mary Ortman process and pasteurize their own cider onsite, and their market store sells apples, produce, homemade baked goods, and meats from local producers. A sign out front promising warm apple dumplings has caused many a driver to hit his brakes! The market is located just 2½ miles north of Monon on State Road 421. It is open Mondays through Fridays from 9:00 AM to 6:00 PM and Saturdays from 9:00 AM to 5:00 PM. It also has seasonal Sunday hours.

Prelock Blueberry Farm

BLUEBERRIES

> 9632 E. 350 S., Lafayette IN 47905 (Tippecanoe)
> www.prelockblueberryfarm.com

The Prelocks have been growing blueberries since the mid-1990s. Years of careful pruning have resulted in bushes that grow some of the largest, most succulent berries in central Indiana. They are an entirely U-Pick operation, and many families pick enough during the season to freeze and last the whole year. The Prelocks do not use chemicals on their berries, so picking is safe for the whole family. During the June blueberry season the farm is open Mondays through Fridays from 7:00 AM to 12 noon and from 4:00 to 8:00 PM and on Saturdays from 7:00 AM to 12 noon. The Prelocks can be contacted via their website.

Purple Rock Farm

POULTRY, BEEF, EGGS

> 2282 East CR 250 N., Frankfort IN 46041 (Clinton)
> 765-659-5310 • www.purplerockfarm.com

Lots of businesses have missions, but Purple Rock Farm takes the concept of a mission to a whole new level. Travis and Gina Sheets sell pastured poultry, highland beef, and farm-fresh eggs to support their work with World Mission Builders, an organization that builds churches in third-world countries and recruits ministerial students to serve in the churches. Their customers not only get great-tasting farm products but also get the satisfaction of supporting World Mission Builders. The Sheetses welcome visitors; call to make arrangements. They've also been known to ask folks to stick around for lunch or dinner!

Red Gold

PROCESSED TOMATO PRODUCTS

Orestes (Madison)
765-754-7527 • www.redgold.com

Red Gold's roots go back to 1942, when Grover Hutcherson and his daughter, Fran, rebuilt a Midwest cannery to provide canned food products for the war effort. The company grew to what we now know as Red Gold, one of the world's largest producers of tomato products. Red Gold grows tomatoes on more than 10,000 acres within 100 miles of the company's central Indiana processing plants. Plant tours are not offered, but Red Gold products are available on nearly every grocery's shelves. If supporting an Indiana food company is important to you, you might want to grab for Red Gold while shopping.

Royer Farm

BEEF, LAMB, PORK

12901 South SR 63, Clinton IN 47842 (Vermillion)
765-832-7104 • www.royerfarmfresh.com

Livestock has been raised on Royer land since 1876, and Scott and Nikki Royer represent the fifth generation to farm it. Their young sons, Cale and Knic, are well on their way to becoming the sixth. This generation of Royers raises beef, lamb, and pork—all pasture-raised without the use of hormones or antibiotics. They utilize local processors, and their beef and lamb are dry-aged to assure full flavor and tenderness. The Royers take orders online and also sell at several farmers' markets, including the Terre Haute Farmers' Market, Broad Ripple Farmers' Market, Zionsville Farmers' Market, and Fishers Farmers' Market. Products are also available on the farm, where hours vary by season.

Spring Creek Farm

PORK, MILK, EGGS

> 1930 E. 850 S., Brookston IN 47923 (White)
> 765-414-5484 • www.springcreekfarm.us

Spring Creek Farm specializes in heritage breeds. One of the farm's signature items is Tamworth pork, which originated in Tamworth, England. Tasting it reveals how much pork has changed over the last few decades. Tamworth pork is succulent, not a word usually used to describe "the other white meat." Pork is available in whole- or half-hog quantities or by the piece, including a wide variety of chops, sausages, roasts, bacon, and more. Spring Creek also sells ground beef from grass-finished cattle, free-range eggs, and "cow shares," which provide the shareholder with a weekly supply of raw, non-homogenized milk. (See "Got Raw Milk?" on p. 148.) Contact Spring Creek via phone or email for more information.

Stegmeier's Sandy Hollow Farm

PRODUCE, EGGS

> 1345 N. Kickapoo Rd., Attica IN 47918 (Fountain)
> 765-764-0819

Karen and Shane Stegmeier practice sustainable and biodynamic agriculture, not using chemicals on their produce or hormones or antibiotics on their animals. They grow some vegetables, fruits, and herbs, but focus mostly on eggs. Their eggs come from laying hens that are range-pastured, eating whatever they find in their natural environment, such as plants, grasses, and insects. Crack open one of the Stegmeiers' eggs and you can instantly see that this omnivorous diet results in deep yellow yolks. A simple scrambled egg from one of their chickens is amazing. Eggs are sold in Lafayette at the River City Depot and at the Lafayette Farmers' Market. Farm visits can be arranged.

Wildflower Ridge Honey Farm

HONEY

> 4217 W. 8th Street Rd., Anderson IN 46011 (Madison)
> 765-641-9972

David Barrickman of Wildflower Ridge Honey is a fourth-generation beekeeper, and thanks to his daughter and grandchildren the family tradition has extended into a fifth and sixth generation. Bees and honey were only a hobby until David retired several years ago and stepped up the operation. Much of his raw, unfiltered honey comes from clover nectar, which produces a light and mild honey. But he also makes the slightly darker and richer wildflower honey. You can often find Wildflower Ridge Honey at farmers' markets and retail outlets. To find out more about Wildflower Ridge products or find a local supplier, give David a call.

"WHAT EXACTLY IS ORGANIC?"

While the question "What exactly is organic?" may seem simple, in reality it is anything but. Long before the term was used on food labels, farming without the use of pesticides and chemical fertilizers was standard procedure.

Then the post–World War II economy brought brand new technologies to agriculture, including ways to boost crop yields and to kill insect pests and weeds with chemicals. Production soared. The U.S., with its affordable and accessible food supply, was the envy of the world. And the technological advances kept coming, along with increases in both efficiency and yield.

There are, however, consequences to many of these technological advances. The changes in the way we grow and process our food have caused changes in our society, our environment, and possibly our health as well. Today more and more people are concerned about the chemicals used in growing and processing our food.

Some home gardeners and a few farmers never adopted the new technologies and just kept right on farming the old-fashioned way, but for several decades the number of customers wanting food grown this way remained small. As consumer concerns about the use of pesticides, herbicides, and synthetic chemical fertilizers have grown, however, so has the number of people willing to pay a little extra for food grown without these technologies. In response, the number of producers willing to alter their production techniques to appeal to this market has also exploded, and the market has also looked increasingly attractive to large-scale agriculture.

Looking for a way to describe food grown without chemicals, producers tried out the word "organic," along with a confusing battery of synonyms like "natural," "whole," "macrobiotic," and "biodiverse." Eventually, the U.S. government stepped in to try to bring some clarity to food labeling. In 1990 Congress passed the Organic Food Production Act, giving the term "organic" a legal definition. In a nutshell, the act requires that products labeled organic must have been produced and processed without synthetic chemicals.

Demand for organic food continues to grow, and organic farming is the fastest-growing segment of agriculture. Giant food companies, recognizing the growing market for the organic label, have mobilized to produce foods that meet the legal definition. Now the term "industrial organic" is part of our food lexicon. Mass production enables these companies to cut their prices far below what small local farmers can usually afford to sell at.

Marketplace competition leaves some small-scale organic farmers struggling to define their value to customers who are shopping exclusively by price, and struggling to decide how they want to use the legal label. While some purists feel that the term "organic" lost some of its value when it was legally defined, other small-scale producers work to qualify for organic certification; others cannot afford to do so, but adhere to organic principles even though they cannot legally use the word. Some farmers reject the government's right to "own" the word when their growing practices would qualify them to use it, and still others, feeling that the legal definition is too lax, consider themselves to be "super-organic."

Our food landscape now includes large non-organic producers, large organic producers, small organic producers who are legally allowed to use the word, and a large group of producers who adopt other terms, like "natural" and "sustainable." Buying local allows customers to query farmers about how their food is grown. The bottom line is that all of us must decide what is important to us about our food supply—taste, price, availability, carbon footprint, workers' conditions, use of synthetic chemicals—and then ask questions and buy accordingly.

EATING LOCAL WHILE DINING OUT

Bonge's Tavern
9830 W. 280 N., Perkinsville IN 46011 (Madison)
765-734-1625 • www.bongestavern.com

Maize: An American Grill
112 N. 3rd St., Lafayette IN 47901 (Tippecanoe)
765-429-6125 • www.maizeinc.com
See p. 82

MCL Anderson
Mounds Mall
2109 SR 9 S., Anderson IN 46016 (Madison)
765-643-2682 • www.mclhomemade.com

MCL Muncie
Muncie Mall
3501 Granville Rd., Muncie IN 47303 (Delaware)
765-289-2955

MCL Richmond
Richmond Square Shopping Center
3801 National Road E., Richmond IN 47374 (Wayne)
765-966-2939

MCL West Lafayette
Wabash Village Center
521 Sagamore Parkway W., West Lafayette IN 47906 (Tippecanoe)
765-463-6621

Mr. Happy Burger
West Location
900 W. Market St., Logansport IN 46947 (Cass)
574-753-4016
See p. 95

Mr. Happy Burger
East Location
3131 E. Market St., Logansport IN 46947 (Cass)
574-753-6418

FARMERS' MARKETS

Centerville Farmers' Market and Country Store
300 N. Morton Ave., Centerville IN 47330 (Wayne)
June–October, Tuesdays through Saturdays 9:00 AM to 5:00 PM

Clinton County Farmers' Market
125 Courthouse Square, Frankfort IN 46041 (Clinton)
May–October, Thursdays 11:00 AM to 5:00 PM,
Saturdays 7:30 AM to 12 noon

Crawfordsville Farmers' Market
100 E. Main St., Crawfordsville IN 47933 (Montgomery)
April–October, Saturdays 8:00 AM to 12 noon

Hartford City Farmers' Market
110 W. Washington St., Hartford City IN 47348 (Blackford)
May 4–October 26, Fridays 4:00 to 7:00 PM

Lafayette Farmers' Market
5th St. between Main and Columbia Streets
Lafayette IN 47901 (Tippecanoe)
May–October, Tuesdays and Saturdays 7:30 AM
to 1:00 PM, Thursdays 4:00 to 7:00 PM
www.lafayettefarmersmarket.com

Logansport Farmers' Market
516 E. Market St., Logansport IN 46947 (Cass)
June–October, Tuesdays and Thursdays 3:00 to
7:00 PM, Saturdays 8:00 AM to 12 noon

Minnetrista Farmers' Market
311 W. Saint Joseph St., Muncie IN 47303 (Delaware)
May–October, Wednesdays 4:00 PM til sold
out, Saturdays 8:00 AM to 12 noon
www.minnetrista.net

Richmond Farmers' Market
Intersection of North 6th and North A Streets
Richmond IN 47374 (Wayne)
June–October, Saturdays 7:00 to 11:00 AM

Sagamore West Farmers' Market
222 N. Chauncey Ave., West Lafayette IN 47906 (Tippecanoe)
May–October, Wednesdays 3:00 to 6:30 PM

Tipton County Farmers' Market
Tipton City parking lot on E. Jefferson St.
Tipton IN 46072 (Tipton)
June–August, Wednesdays 4:00 to 8:00 PM,
    Saturdays 8:00 AM to 12 noon

WINERIES

New Day Meadery
701 S. Anderson St., Elwood IN 46036 (Madison)
765-552-3433 • www.newdaymeadery.com
See p. 85

Oak Hill Winery
111 E. Marion St., Converse IN 46919 (Miami)
765-395-3632 • www.oakhillwines.com

Wilson Winery
10137 S. Indian Trail Rd., Modoc IN 47358 (Randolph)
765-853-5100 • www.wilsonwines.com

Whyte Horse Winery
1510 S. Airport Rd., Monticello IN 47960 (White)
574-583-2345 • www.whytehorsewinery.com

MICROBREWERIES & BREWPUBS

Half Moon Restaurant Brewery
4051 S. Lafountain St., Kokomo IN 46902 (Howard)
765-455-2739 • www.halfmoonbrewery.com

Lafayette Brewing
622 Main St., Lafayette IN 47901 (Tippecanoe)
765-742-2592 • www.lafayettebrewingco.com

North Central Indiana

FOOD FESTIVALS

Elwood Red Gold Chili Cook-Off
Unique and tasty cooking competitions
Elwood IN (Madison)
Mid-October
765-552-0180 • www.elwoodchamber.org

Frankfort Hot Dog Festival
Hot dogs with all kinds of toppings
Frankfort IN (Clinton)
End of July
765-654-4081 • www.mainstreet.accs.net

Kokomo Rib Fest
BBQ of all sorts
Kokomo IN (Howard)
Mid-June
765-423-2787

Kokomo Strawberry Festival
Kokomo IN (Howard)
Fresh strawberries and strawberry shortcake
Early June
765-454-7926

Mansfield Village Cornbread Festival
Freshly baked cornbread, ham and beans, chili, and stew
Mansfield IN (Parke)
Early September
765-653-4026 • www.MansfieldVillage.com

Mansfield Village Maple Festival
Mansfield IN (Parke)
Pancakes with maple syrup and other foods
Late February/Early March
765-653-4026 • www.MansfieldVillage.com

Mansfield Village Mushroom Festival
Mushrooms bought, sold, traded, and eaten
Mansfield IN (Parke)
Late April
765-653-4026 • www.MansfieldVillage.com

Mansfield Village Watermelon Festival
Watermelon and other foods
Mansfield IN (Parke)
Mid-August
765-653-4026 • www.mansfieldvillage.com

Parke County Maple Fair
Pancakes with maple syrup and other foods
Late February/Early March
Rockville IN (Parke)
765-569-5226 • www.ParkeCounty.com

Strawberry Festival
Strawberries and ice cream, shortcake, and crepes
Crawfordsville IN (Montgomery)
Early June
800-866-3973 • www.thestrawberryfestival.com

Tipton County Pork Festival
BBQ pork chops and other foods
Tipton IN (Tipton)
Early September
765-675-2342 • www.tiptoncountyporkfestival.com

Van Buren Popcorn Festival
Popcorn-related food, crafts, and activities
Van Buren IN (Grant)
2nd week of August
765-934-4888 • www.jerrypalmer.com/vanburen/popcorn

YWCA Strawberry Festival
Strawberry shortcake
Early June
Lafayette IN (Tippecanoe)
765-742-0075 • www.ywca.org/lafayette

North Central Indiana

4

Home Grown Indiana

108

Central

"Central Indiana," as defined in this book, includes Marion County and the surrounding seven counties of Boone, Hamilton, Hancock, Hendricks, Johnson, Morgan, and Shelby—the "donut" counties, if you will. Read carefully and you may even find an actual donut or two in these central Indiana pages! The locally grown food scene around Indianapolis is vibrant and exciting, with working farms only a few miles from the center of the city supplying homes and restaurants with fabulous fresh food. Central Indiana food producers range from those that have been around for a century to those of a much more recent vintage, and from large establishments to smaller mom-and-pop-type places. You don't need to wander far from the city to find some amazing food.

Apple Family Farm

DAIRY, EGGS, CHICKEN, BEEF, AND LAMB

3365 West SR 234, McCordsville IN 46055 (Hancock)
317-335-3067 • www.applefamilyfarm.com

The family farm in McCordsville, just east of Indianapolis, is a far cry from the bright lights of the Nashville music industry in which Debbie and Mark Apple used to make their living, but neither seems to regret leaving the glitz and glamour behind. In fact, they and their kids, Brayden and Rhayna, are thriving on the farm, where they are the third and fourth generations to work the land. These most recent Apples take an all-natural approach to raising their pastured chickens, sheep, and beef and dairy cows, eschewing the use of chemicals, antibiotics, or growth hormones.

Anyone who has read Joel Salatin's books on innovative farming methods will recognize the mobile chicken coops out in the Apples' fields. The chickens aren't allowed to roam freely for fear of predators, but the coops give them plenty of legroom and lots of choice morsels to peck up from the ground as they follow in the wake of the cows who grazed there a few days before. The farming here is sustainable and contained—the goal is to provide everything the animals need from the farm itself (though droughts and other hazards of nature can make that impossible at times). The Apples believe not only that such farming is kinder to the environment, but that the resulting eggs and meat will taste much better and be healthier for people to consume.

There are hardly any downsides to sustainable agriculture practiced this way, except that it is labor-intensive and the yields aren't as great as they can be when farmers crowd their animals together, pump them full of growth hormones to fatten them quickly, and slaughter them early. It also doesn't generate as much money as farmers can sometimes make by selling their land to developers eager to turn it into suburban sprawl—Apple Family Farm is now a lonely oasis of fields in the midst of new construction and real-estate signs.

The Apples remain undaunted in their commitment to sustainable agriculture, however, and they have big plans. Their onsite Farm Market is a super place to shop for meats (chicken, dry-aged highland beef, and pasture-raised lamb and veal) and dairy products, including eggs, butter, and the raw milk cheeses made by Swiss Connection (see p. 168) Their School of Farming and Homesteading offers classes in food preservation, cheese making, weaving, hands-on farming techniques, and other subjects near to the Apples' heart. As well, they sell cow shares; part-owners of a cow can obtain fresh raw milk on the farm (see "Got Raw Milk?" on p. 148).

The farm offers tours tailored to interested adults as well as more kid-friendly visits (see the website for information), and the Farm Market is open daily. The Apples also sell at the Traders Point Creamery Farmers' Market.

Double T Venison Ranch

VENISON, ELK, AND BISON MEATS

> 2913 Hollow Branch Rd., Martinsville IN 46151 (Morgan)
> 888-349-1889 • www.venisondeerfarmer.com

Visiting the Double T Ranch in Martinsville is like straying into Dr. Doolittle land. Two furious white geese may sound the alarm for your arrival, honking and flapping furiously. Their racket will disperse a couple of wild turkeys and summon a friendly pup who trots out, tail wagging, to see what's up. Just standing around placidly amid all this hullabaloo are the whole point of the operation—crowds of small, watchful, almost delicate-looking deer. Human beings don't usually get to see deer that aren't fleeing from them in heart-pounding fear. These little guys gaze at you, munching leaves, strolling up to the fence, looking a little wary, a little interested, but not afraid. No adrenalin rush, no fuss, not even much curiosity.

For Tim Tague, rancher and owner of the Double T, deer farming is close to his heart. "I am passionate about it, just passionate about it," he says, nodding his head sharply in emphasis. A longtime hunter, Tague had origi- nally dreamed of running the Double T as a high-fence hunting operation. Traveling around the country to see how such places work, however, gave him pause, as he saw that some hunters behaved differently and, in his view, unethically when hunting fenced animals. Knowing he'd have limited control over his clientele, he changed his plans and went into deer farming instead.

At the core of Tague's ranching philosophy is a deep affection for his animals. Being a hunter doesn't mean you can't be an animal lover, he explains. In fact, you may love them more as you come to know so much about them— their nature and their habits. But he is no sentimentalist, either. He finds it entirely natural to raise the deer, give them an idyllic, protected life for a few years, and then harvest them, as he calls it, to provide wholesome nutri- tion for human beings. There is a natural order to this business that strikes him as right.

Farm-raised venison is not the tough and gamey meat that some people expect. The flavor is surprisingly mild, rich, and what Tague calls "woodsy." The Double T sells all cuts of venison—ribs, steaks, and roasts—as well as jerky, snack sticks, sausage, and, as he says, "Pretty much anything else you could want from a deer." Elk and buffalo meat are also available.

Double T products are available at the Bloomington Winter Farmers' Market and at Bloomingfoods. The Country Store at the ranch is open Saturdays and Sundays from 1:00 to 5:00 PM and other times by arrangement. The Double T offers child-friendly farm tours in the spring, when the fawns are born. Special events include lessons on cooking game and special lectures. Call or check the website for details.

Elements

RESTAURANT

415 N. Alabama St., Indianapolis IN 46204 (Marion)
317-634-8888 • www.elementsindy.com

Greg Hardesty, chef and owner of Elements, is a solid, soft-spoken man, whose voice gradually warms with passion as he talks about food and the challenges involved in presenting the highest-quality ingredients in the simplest, most delicious way possible. The cooking at Elements is, well, elemental. Showing the Japanese and French influences in his training, Hardesty manipulates the food as little as he can, and nothing goes on the plate that is not meant to be eaten. No froufrou garnishes here or unwieldy herb branches; Hardesty is a food purist, and a minimalist at heart.

Working with food was not Hardesty's first career choice. Graduating from Indiana University with a degree in public affairs, he tried selling vinyl siding and insurance, only to reach the firm conviction that he wasn't a salesperson. He had enjoyed working in a restaurant in his Bloomington days, so he went to work at the Glass Chimney in Indianapolis, learning classic continental food preparation. Newly married and ready for a change, he moved to Los Angeles and began work in the restaurant empire of Joachim Splichal. There he learned the ethic of California freshness overlaid with a Mediterranean influence, and picked up a fondness for cooking with olive oil (not, he says with a smile, that there isn't a time and a place for using lots of butter as well).

Today, all the food in his elegant downtown Indianapolis restaurant is natural and made from scratch, and ingredients are local where possible. Hardesty's quest for the highest-quality ingredients has led him to seek out local producers who can provide the fine meats, produce, and cheeses that his elemental cuisine requires. Buying local appeals to him for environmental reasons, but also because local food is fresher and tastier. He says, "There's just something about produce that is still a bit warm from the sun that gets me excited!" His food sources include Your Neighbor's Garden, Seldom Seen Farm, Fischer Farm, Melody Acres, Homestead Growers, Capriole Farms, Traders Point, Hickoryworks, and others.

Depending on the season, diners looking for dishes based on local ingredients at Elements might find a Salad of Indiana Tomatoes, Pine Nuts, Arugula, and Traders Point Creamery Fleur de la Terre Cheese with Sherry Vinaigrette; Braised Fischer Farms Pork Cheeks with Smoky Savoy Cabbage and Red Wine Pork Braise; or a Warm Peach Tart with Cinnamon Ice Cream and Shagbark Hickory Syrup. The menu changes frequently and is posted on the website, so check for updates.

AMISH CHICKEN WITH GARDEN VEGETABLE RAGOUT

Chef Greg Hardesty uses chicken grown on Indiana Amish farms and vegetables straight from the garden. This is one of those 30-minute meals perfect for a weeknight supper.

- 6 chicken breasts, boneless with skin on
- 5 tablespoons olive oil
- 1 large onion, julienned
- 2 garlic cloves, minced
- 3 roasted red peppers, peeled and julienned
- 3 roasted yellow or green peppers, peeled and julienned
- 2 jalapeños, seeded and sliced thin
- ¼ cup niçoise olives, halved
- 4 Roma tomatoes, peeled, seeded, and julienned
- ½ cup chicken stock
- 1 teaspoon red wine vinegar
- 2 cups spinach leaves
- Salt and pepper to taste

Preheat oven to 400°. Heat 2 tablespoons olive oil over medium-high heat in an oven-proof pan. Season chicken breast with salt and pepper and place in the pan, skin side down. Cook for 2 minutes. Place pan in oven and cook for 6–8 minutes, until chicken is just cooked through. Remove chicken from oven and place on a plate to rest for three minutes, lightly covered with aluminum foil.

In the same pan, heat 2 tablespoons olive oil over medium heat and add onions. Sauté for 2 minutes until just beginning to brown, then add garlic and continue to cook another minute. Add peppers, tomatoes, olives, and chicken stock to pan. Cook until reduced by half. Add remaining tablespoon olive oil, red wine vinegar, and spinach leaves and cook until spinach is just wilted. Add any accumulated chicken juices from resting plate. Season ragout with salt and pepper to taste. Ladle into 6 bowls and top each with a chicken breast. Serves 6.

Hickoryworks

SYRUPS

3615 Peoga Rd., Trafalgar IN 46181 (Johnson)
317-878-5648 • www.hickoryworks.com

When Gordon Jones and Sherrie Yarling decided to leave their home in southern Florida in search of falling leaves and four authentic seasons, they did a kind of reverse Beverly Hillbillies, hitching their Cadillac to a trailer and moving to Yarling family property in the far reaches of Indiana hill country. Once there, they spent several years in the shiitake mushroom–growing business before fate intervened in the guise of an elderly stranger who stopped by one day. Listening to him recall how his great-great-grandmother had made syrup from the bark of Brown County shagbark hickory trees, Jones and Yarling were inspired to give syrup making a try.

These days they're kept busy producing both shagbark hickory syrup and poplar syrup, as well as a luscious barbeque sauce. When they aren't making syrup they're on the road promoting and selling their wares, or at home maintaining an elaborate website and handling their mail-order business.

Chatting with Jones and Yarling can leave you breathless yourself, as they trade reminiscences, finish each other's sentences, and happily follow each other down conversational trails that may or may not find their way back to the original destination. They glance off many subjects—the well-known chefs who use their syrup; how they got the upscale New York store Dean & Deluca to carry their products; how the Food Network taped a segment on their syrup; and what happens when *Gourmet* or *Midwest Living* unexpectedly runs a story about you and you find yourself with 3500 orders to fill and only two of you to fill them. They tell their life story as a glorious, quirky adventure full of surprises, successes, and interesting people, and they want their listeners to enjoy it as much as they do.

They want them to enjoy the syrup too, even if it is a bit hard to describe to someone who has never tasted it. When Ronni Lundy wrote in *Gourmet* about her excitement at finding the syrup that had become legendary in her childhood, she described it as having a bit of a "whang." Whatever that is, shagbark hickory syrup certainly has it. No mellow golden maple syrup here. Sipped from a spoon, it has an edge. You take a bite and it bites you back.

But that is the syrup in a spoon, straight up. Add it to the right food, and it is transformed into an unimaginable gustatory pleasure. Lundy suggests pouring it over corncakes, and there are plenty of other suggestions in the Hickoryworks cookbook, available on the website. Try sweet potato fries with shagbark syrup or the Shagbark Cheesecake (see p. 84).

Hickoryworks is not open to the public, but you can order Shagbark Hickory Syrup directly from the Hickoryworks website or from Dean & Deluca (though that's pricier), or buy it at Oliver Winery or at Meijer stores in central Indiana.

Homestead Growers

MUSHROOMS, PRODUCE, CSA

> 25325 Lamong Rd., Sheridan IN 46069 (Hamilton)
> 317-727-2730 • www.homestead-growers.com

Steve Spencer of Homestead Growers is the Mushroom Man, selling at farmers' markets all over central Indiana. He harvests a colorful bounty of eggplants, tomatoes, squash, and onions, all grown on the 30 acres of family farmland he shares with his brother in Sheridan, where they are the sixth generation of the family to work that land. But it's the huge cooler of mushrooms behind his market stand that really draws market-goers year-round.

Like so many farmers today, Spencer didn't always dream of being one, despite the existence of the family homestead. He spent years in the furniture business before falling in love with the idea of mushroom farming and coming home to the land. Now that he has, he is intent on making a living for his family from his efforts, becoming a farmer entrepreneur in his determination to grow the business and find new ways to market his products.

It all began with mushrooms. The Spencer family has always had a passion for mushrooms, hunting morels in the woods every spring. When Steve talked to a friend who had bought a mushroom-growing business in Florida, he was instantly smitten with the idea, so much so that he and his brother built a similar facility on the family farm. They've been growing shiitakes and oysters since 2000, and added criminis and portabellas in 2006. At the same time, they grow a huge variety of chemical-free, all-natural produce.

And now the Spencers are making it easy, even for the time-pressed or kitchen-challenged among us, to enjoy the fruits of their harvest. Under the label Local Folks Food, they have turned their mushroom mania, as well as the other products of their farm, into a business, working with area chefs and the people at the Ohio River Valley Food Venture in Madison (see p. 248) to create mushroom patties (excellent sautéed in olive oil and served up on a bun, with mayonnaise, lettuce, tomato, and onion) and a rich mushroom and vegetable pasta sauce. They also make ravioli (one kind filled with butternut squash, and another with mushrooms and a touch of blue cheese), and future plans include a variety of pickled mushrooms and soups, including mushroom barley. Local Folks products use produce from Homestead Growers as well as other area growers.

Homestead Growers produce and products are available at farmers' markets in Bloomington, Broad Ripple, Carmel, Fishers, Goshen, Indianapolis (three different markets!), and Noblesville, as well as through the farm's own CSA (see "What Is a CSA?" on p. 180). See the website for details. Some markets, like Bloomington's, allow only products made entirely by the vendors to be sold, so not all the Spencers' processed foods may be on sale there, but mushroom patties are usually available.

Indianapolis City Market

MEATS, PRODUCE, BAKED GOODS

> 222 E. Market St., Indianapolis IN 46204 (Marion)
> 317-632-9266 • www.indianapoliscitymarket.org

In 1821 Alexander Ralston, the man who plotted the town of Indianapolis, parceled out a small piece of land for use as a market. A small building was constructed on the site for the sale of meat and produce. In 1896 a much larger building was constructed to house retail and produce stands and to accommodate public events like political rallies and concerts. The City Market was a regular destination for urban Hoosiers. It was a convenient, under-one-roof location for fresh produce, meat, fish, poultry, and dairy and bakery goods. Many people new to Indiana or even to the U.S. established businesses at the market, bringing exotic foods from far-away lands to native Hoosiers.

After World War II, when suburbia became the American dream, grocery stores popped up on the outskirts of town and the City Market felt the impact of competition. But after a couple decades of decline, the late '60s and the '70s saw reinvestment in the facility. The buildings were renovated and retailers began to repopulate the space. Lost, however, was the connection to Indiana agriculture. The food vendors were making terrific sandwiches and other foods but the fresh-from-the-farm meats and produce that were once the centerpiece of the market were a distant memory.

To help reconnect the city to the farm, City Market leaders began an outdoor farmers' market. Open on Wednesdays from 10:00 AM to 1:30 PM, May through October, it is the largest farmers' market in Indianapolis, with nearly 40 vendors. Now summer Wednesdays take on a festival atmosphere, with live music and city folks visiting with country folks. People who work downtown, even those who commute from the suburbs, look forward to the market.

A couple of years ago, the City Market leadership decided to make the farm-to-city connection even stronger with another renovation that would help bring Indiana-produced meats, produce, and other goods back into the market. Now local vendors like Moody Meats, Constantine's Italian Produce, and others sell their wares at the indoor market six days a week throughout the year. The Wednesday outdoor farmers' market continues, but downtown residents and commuters alike now have a place to get fresh meats, fruits, and vegetables every day, and new relationships are developing between farmers and city chefs. Shoppers can pick up a couple of steaks from Moody Meats, some vegetables from Constantine's, and a loaf of freshly baked bread all under one roof. The one-stop shop originally envisioned in the 1800s is once again a reality. The Indianapolis City Market is emerging as Indiana's urban hub for local foods.

And the future looks even brighter for the Indianapolis City Market. Plans are in the works for an onsite restaurant that will specialize in cuisine prepared from the best of Indiana's farm products. The restaurant will serve breakfast, lunch, and dinner.

The Indianapolis City Market is open Mondays through Fridays from 6:00 AM to 4:00 PM and Saturdays from 11:00 AM to 3:00 PM, although the hours of individual merchants may vary.

Joe's Butcher Shop and Fish Market

BEEF, PORK, CHICKEN, SEAFOOD

> 111 W. Main St., Carmel IN 46032 (Hamilton)
> 317-846-8877 • www.joesbutchershop.com

The people of Carmel may or may not have a good baker or candlestick maker, but one thing for sure is that they have a terrific butcher. In January 2006, Joe Lazzara dropped out of the corporate rat race to open this throwback meat and fish shop in Carmel's trendy Arts and Design District. In this labor of love, Lazzara enlisted the help of Fritz Albright, a veteran butcher who for 30 years had had a successful shop near Fort Wayne. Joe, his wife Kathy, and Fritz have done a great job mixing the traditional with the contemporary, and Joe's may be the only place in Indiana where you can get both a top-notch Porterhouse and sashimi-grade ahi tuna.

A few decades ago, many people bought their meat from a local butcher with whom they were on a first-name-basis. In contrast, the meat at many of today's supermarkets arrives already cut and wrapped in plastic; even when a meat cutter is on hand, he is usually well hidden. And when it comes to buying meat, what you see is what you get. Part of the pleasure of shopping at Joe's is that you get Nordstrom-like customer service from Joe, Fritz, and the rest of the gang. Special requests, preparation tips, and general small talk are part of the standard operating procedure. And there are few things more satisfying to a meat lover than a slow, mouth-watering walk down the full length of Joe's display case, eying a well-marbled, bone-in ribeye; a double-thick pork chop; and short ribs just waiting for a slow braise. An armful of packages wrapped in thick white butcher's paper can render a carnivore as positively giddy as a three-year-old on Christmas morning.

The shop carries a full line of beef, pork, and chicken. The all-natural chicken comes from Indiana Amish and Mennonite farms and is available whole, in parts, and in the ever popular boneless, skinless breasts. The pork, also from Indiana farms, is available in a wide variety of cuts as well as in the form of house-made sausages. Joe's quality beef comes from Nebraska and it is available in any cut imaginable. The whole beef tenderloin is especially popular.

The fresh seafood selections change daily. The shop follows the Monterey Bay Aquarium's Seafood Watch Program, which ensures that Joe's fish and seafood is sustainably caught or farmed. The fish and seafood choices are not as varied as the meats, but discriminating shoppers can be sure that all them are flown in daily and guaranteed to be fresh and delicious.

The meat and fish are certainly the main attraction at Joe's, but there are lots of supporting characters—loads of sauces and marinades, a nice selection of cheeses, a few well-selected wines, and other odds and ends are available as well. You can turn to Joe Lazzara for everything from a special-occasion whole beef tenderloin to weekday-supper chicken breasts, and everything will be top-notch.

Lazzara also offers two special customer service packages, a Prime account and a Choice account. Customers with Prime accounts can place orders online or by fax as well as in the store, can pick them up curbside or have them delivered, and have access to exclusive specials by email. Holders of Choice accounts have fewer options, but still get first-rate customer service. Joe's is open seven days a week, with shorter hours on Sunday.

Moody Meats and Lone Pine Farms

BEEF, PORK, CHICKEN, EGGS

> Indianapolis City Market
> 222 E. Market St., Indianapolis IN 46204 (Marion)
> 317-687-1901
>
> 9348 S. 550 E., Ladoga IN 47954 (Montgomery)
> 765-942-2442
>
> 235 North SR 267, Avon IN 46123 (Hendricks)
> 317-272-4533 • www.moodymeats.com

Adam Moody's family farm and meat business is a cornerstone of central Indiana's local food scene. With the farm operation, a network of additional local beef producers, and three retail locations, the Moodys have set the standard for locally raised and processed poultry, pork, and beef.

The story began way back in 1871 when Lone Pine Farms began operation in the flatlands of southern Montgomery County. Adam's grandfather, Oscar Moody, began working the farm in the 1920s and purchased it in 1952. The farm is now in the hands of Adam and his father Dennis. In 1987 the Moodys began farming sustainably without using chemicals, and in 1997 they began transitioning their corn and soybean fields to the production of chicken, eggs, beef, and pork. For the first few years, Adam and his wife, Lucy, sold their goods at central Indiana farmers' markets. In 2000 they took the bold step of opening a retail location in Ladoga. They have now added a retail location in Avon and were the first tenants of the revamped Indianapolis City Market.

A farm operation and three retail locations require plenty of dedicated people to keep operations humming along. All six of the Moodys' kids are part of the family business, representing the sixth generation to be involved in the evolving enterprise.

The Moody philosophy is to focus first on faith and family and then on employees and customers—a business philosophy that begins with the family farm and then ends at the family dinner table. According to Adam, their standards go far beyond the government definition of "organic." Their products are all-natural, without added hormones or antibiotics.

Moody Meats sells beef from Lone Pine Farms and other nearby Indiana farms. Nearly every cut imaginable is available. When it looks as though demand for certain prime cuts will outpace supply, Adam works with an Indiana broker to bring in Midwest beef raised according to the standards he insists on. Ground beef is popular as well. It is 92–94 percent lean and Moody Meats sells lots of it—more than 4,000 pounds per week. Some specialty burgers are also available, including Onion Burgers and the popular Bacon Burger, with hickory-smoked bacon ground right in.

Promised Land Farm

TURKEY

9781 W. 275 N., Thorntown IN 46071 (Boone)
765-483-9268 • www.promisedlandfarm.us

The main attraction at most Thanksgiving dinners is the turkey. The Norman Rockwell image of the roasted bird, carved at the table, is as American an icon as any we have. But as big a star as the Thanksgiving turkey is, the way most of us get it is anything but special. A trip to the mega-market early in the week yields all our holiday food-stuffs, including a bird frozen hard as a rock. A couple of days in the fridge to thaw and we're good to go, giving as much thought to Tom Turkey as to the canned green beans in our crispy onion-topped casserole.

For about 175 families in central Indiana, however, buying a turkey is a very different experience. Jim and Nancy Wheland's Promised Land Farm in Thorntown specializes in all-natural, pasture-raised turkeys. Each February the small poults, or young fowl, arrive on the farm, where Jim tells them about their special purpose in life—to help families have a very special Thanksgiving. Throughout the year, visitors can stop by to see the turkeys doing what turkeys do best—running around, eating, enjoying the shade, and gobbling to each other about whatever turkeys gobble to each other about.

Near the end of the week before Thanksgiving, they are taken out for processing and are back at the farm the Saturday before the holiday for families to pick up. For these families, Thanksgiving has an added dimension. They know where their birds came from, they've shaken the hands of those who cared for them, and they are as-sured that their turkey lived a good life. They thus have even more to be thankful for.

The turkey business is not what initially brought the Whelands to the farm. They originally dreamed of just keeping a few sheep so their beloved herding dogs, Brody and Taffy, could sharpen their skills. Goats and chickens soon followed, and then they thought of selling turkeys as a way to share their "promised land" with others. Brody and Taffy have passed on, but four other dogs now occupy their place on the farm and visitors can often see them in action, putting the sheep through their paces.

After looking at the various ways of raising turkeys, the Whelands decided on the day range method. This means that the turkeys spend their nights in their pen for protection from predators, and each morning the Whelands let them out to roam the farm until bedtime. As for how they taste, repeat customers tell the story. "Succulent," "juicy," and "just more turkey-like" are some of the comments they have made. Some, traveling out of town for Thanksgiving, have even iced their Promised Land birds down and taken them across the country.

Those interested in a turkey for Thanksgiving can visit the Promised Land website to place an order. Visits to the farm can be arranged by giving the Whelands a call.

R bistro

RESTAURANT

888 Massachusetts Ave., Indianapolis IN 46202 (Marion)
317-423-0312 • www.rbistro.com

Chef Regina Mehallick of R bistro came late to cooking, and it's clear she relishes her midlife career change. At the age of 35, she quit managing medical offices and went to study cooking at Johnson and Wales University in South Carolina, where her husband's job had taken them. Moving again, across the Atlantic this time, she honed her craft in British restaurants and Irish cooking classes.

All the ingredients used in her classes at Ballymaloe, in County Cork, were fresh—the herbs and lettuces were picked straight from the garden, and the free-range eggs, chickens, fish, and lamb were all local. Mehallick was struck by how much better these things tasted, and since for her food is all about taste, she was hooked on the philosophy of using local products.

She brought that philosophy with her when, having moved to Indiana on her return to the States, she decided it was time to open her own place. She was 47 years old and thought, "I'm old enough, and if I don't do it now, I never will. Some things in your life you just need to try."

Finding the right space was difficult. She eventually settled on an old castor factory with high brick walls, which has been transformed into a tour de force of chrome, color, and light. Just as difficult was finding the local purveyors she had come to rely on in Ireland and Scotland. Today her food is as fresh and local as she can get it: she buys from local mushroom growers and fish farmers as well as from the meat and vegetable producers she has found.

Her cooking is essential and spare, so that the fine ingredients she chooses can shine through. There are no frills or furbelows, no fancy architecture or gimmicks. She cooks meat and fish simply, with oil, salt, and pepper, and concentrates on accompaniments to enhance what's on the plate. It is minimalist cooking, with a premium on taste and quality.

At R bistro, the menu of five appetizers, five entrees, and five desserts changes weekly—a tremendous challenge for the kitchen staff. Mehallick is constantly reading, thinking, brainstorming with her chefs, and checking what ingredients are available to come up with ideas for the menu. She finalizes ideas by Saturday, places her orders on Monday, gets all the food in on Tuesday, and starts a new menu every Wednesday. By Saturday, they have finally gotten it all down right, and then they change the menu again and start all over.

This extraordinarily ambitious undertaking is possible only because of teamwork. She values her talented staff and lists them by name, cooks and servers alike, on her menu, along with the names of the local producers she buys her food from. Why not credit everyone, she says? After all, it's a collaborative effort. That kind of generosity of spirit is reflected throughout the restaurant, and makes dining there a pleasure.

SUMMER VEGETABLE STEW

According to Chef Regina Mehallick, this Summer Vegetable Stew is delicious served over just about any starch. A particular favorite is a medley of brown, wild, and basmati rice, each cooked separately and then combined along with a little butter, some orange zest, ground coriander, and salt to taste. Raid the farmers' market or the backyard garden for a vegetarian feast.

- 1 onion, diced
- 3 garlic cloves, minced
- ¼ cup extra-virgin olive oil
- 2 medium zucchini, diced (3 cups)
- 1 medium yellow squash, diced (1½ cups)
- 1 red bell pepper, chopped
- 1 cup fresh corn kernels (about 2 ears' worth)
- 2 tomatoes, diced
- 2 tablespoons minced fresh oregano leaves
- ½ cup packed shredded fresh basil leaves

In a large, deep skillet cook the onion and garlic in the oil over moderately low heat, stirring, until softened. Add zucchini, yellow squash, pepper, and corn and cook over moderate heat, stirring, for 4 minutes. Add tomatoes, oregano, and salt and pepper to taste and simmer, covered, 10 minutes, stirring occasionally. Uncover and simmer 5 more minutes, or until excess liquid has evaporated. Remove from heat and cool. To serve, reheat and add the fresh basil at the last moment. Serves 4–6.

Seldom Seen Farm

PRODUCE AND HERBS

2525 N. 425 E., Danville IN 46122 (Hendricks)
317-509-7828 • www.seldomseenfarm.com

In 2001, tired of traveling around the country and unable to settle on a trade, John Feree came home to the family farm, 160 acres in central Hendricks County. Determined to find a way to make a living that didn't require commuting, he read everything he could find on sustainable, low-impact market farming and interned at a farm in Illinois. In 2004 he was ready to strike out on his own, creating Seldom Seen Farm out of 10 acres of transitional organic farmland.

Today he and Kelly Funk grow vegetables, flowers, and lots and lots of salad mix on the land. They produce pea shoots, scallions, broccoli, cabbage, carrots, heirloom tomatoes, cherry tomatoes, red peppers, asparagus, arugula, mizuna, tatsoi, spinach, basil, cucumbers, squash, kale, mustards, turnips, and radishes. Salad mix is their primary product year-round, amounting to about 50 percent of their gross sales, and they are one of the few volume producers of salad mix in Indianapolis. They sell their produce at area markets and to more than seven Indianapolis restaurants. If you've had a salad at Elements, L'Explorateur, Oceanaire, Oh Yumm! Bistro, Taste Café, or Traders Point Creamery Café, chances are you've eaten Seldom Seen greens.

Creating a viable business from an activity that he has felt called to in part for ideological reasons ("because the optimistic side of me would like to see humanity evolve, leaving behind the exploitation, abuse, and anthropocentrism that has been our foundation for 10,000 years") is a challenge. Do you keep it small-scale and do all the farm labor, selling, and business management yourself, or do you expand, hiring employees who then have to be managed and supervised? When Feree's mom told him he was becoming "quite the capitalist," he wondered if he was getting the balance wrong. But the need to make a living by farming limits his choices, and finding the right business plan remains a struggle even as he has scaled back.

In addition to selling to restaurants, at the Traders Point and Broad Ripple markets, and at Bloomington's Winter Market, Feree and Funk have opened a Farm Market on their land. The market is open on Thursday evenings June through September, from 4:00 to 8:00 PM.

Skillington Farms

CHICKEN, PORK, AND BEEF

465 N. 500 E., Lebanon IN 46052 (Boone)
765-482-5481 • www.skillingtonfarms.com

"I know a guy." Mob stories seem to always have a character who utters this bit of dialogue, someone who is, as they say, "connected." When the situation calls for a dentist on the take, he says, "Hey, I know a guy"; or when someone has an item to dispose of, maybe a six-foot, 200-pound item in the trunk of a car, it's "Fugeddaboutit, I know a guy."

One of the great things about eating local is that you too can become "connected," though certainly not in a Mafia way. When someone asks you where to find a great farmstead cheese, you know a guy. Persimmon pulp? You know a guy. When it comes to great pasture-raised chicken, pork, and beef in central Indiana, a growing number of people can say, "Hey, I know a guy," and that guy is Stan Skillington.

Skillington got a taste of farming early in life, helping out on a friend's farm. As he later carved out a successful high-tech career and started a family, the idea of a life on the farm still lingered somewhere in the back of his mind. When they had the opportunity to buy some land on the outskirts of Lebanon, the Skillingtons decided to get in touch with their inner agrarians. As Stan researched various types of farming, he became interested in the production practices of Joel Salatin. Over the last seven years, he has adopted and adapted many of Salatin's methods and added his own innovations, providing a growing number of food-conscious central Indiana families with all-natural beef, pork, and poultry produced without hormones, antibiotics, growth stimulants, or animal byproducts in the feed.

It only takes a few minutes of talking with Skillington to be impressed with his passion and ingenuity. New customers usually find Skillington Farms through recommendations by his regular customers. They report that his chicken is absolutely delicious—moist, tender, and much more flavorful than the typical grocery-store bird. Pair his smoky and not-too-salty bacon with some farm-fresh eggs and you've got a breakfast to remember. First-timers might walk away from their first visit with no more than a couple of whole chickens, some ground beef, and a pound of bacon, but before long they are putting a freezer in the garage and filling it with his wholesome meat and poultry. His pork and beef go fast, so preorders are recommended. Stan processes several times each year and his products can be picked up on the farm.

The Skillingtons love to provide tours for schoolkids and other groups, and there will soon be lots more to see on the farm. Plans for the near future include a federally approved processing facility that will allow them to produce even more chickens, a customer service center, and a commercial kitchen. The next time you are asked about local chicken, beef, or pork, you can say, "Hey, I know a guy!" Call to arrange a visit.

Traders Point Creamery

DAIRY, BEEF, RESTAURANT

> 9101 Moore Rd., Zionsville IN 46077 (Boone)
> 317-773-1700 • www.tpforganics.com

In case you were thinking that chocolate milk is just a kid thing, think again. The chocolate milk at Traders Point Creamery is a grown-up fantasy—a dreamy, creamy concoction of dense Dutch cocoa and rich whole dairy milk. Of course, the smooth and fruity yogurt is pretty darn good too, and so is the ice cream, and the cheeses, both fresh and aged, are something really special.

Although many Traders Point Creamery products are now available in grocery stores around central Indiana (and elsewhere in the country in Whole Foods stores), the creamery is well worth a visit. Although it's a quick drive from the center of Indianapolis, this bucolic farm is worlds away from the city in every other respect. Jane and Fritz Kuntz, with some talented help, have turned the family farm into an oasis of sustainable agriculture, state-of-the-art cheese making, and just plain good eating.

The farm motto is "Nourish the land that nourishes us all," and that sums up the Kuntz's philosophy of farming. Their Brown Swiss cows are grass-fed and USDA-certified organic, meaning that they are raised without antibiotics or synthetic hormones and the grass they feed on is pesticide-free. Keeping the cows happy and healthy is the job of New Zealander Neil McDonald. Neil's goal is to give the cows the best life they can have, with plenty of fresh air, good grass to eat, and soft earth to lie on. In return, happy, healthy cows will produce wholesome, delicious milk.

Traders Point milk is not homogenized. Homogenization is a process by which commercial milk producers extend the shelf life of milk by breaking up the fat globules that make it creamy into tiny bits, so that they stay suspended in the milk and the milk thus stays fresh longer. Modern milk manufacturing immediately separates out the fat, breaks it up, and adds it back in the desired proportion—whole milk is 3.5 percent fat, and other varieties may be 2 or 1 percent fat, or entirely skim. In non-homogenized, creamline milk, the fat globules do not stay suspended, and eventually they rise to the top. The lucky people who get the first pour out of a bottle of creamline milk get a rich and creamy treat. This layer of cream can also be skimmed off the top and used separately, or shaken back into the milk.

The man in charge of turning Traders Point milk into fabulous dairy products is Fons Smits, who came to Zionsville from his native Holland by way of places like Mongolia, Tanzania, and California. Smits, who has a degree in dairy sciences, created the Creamery's wonderful chocolate milk, the award-winning fruit yogurts, the fresh cheeses, and the aged cheese Fleur de la Terre (which recently won a blue ribbon from the American Cheese Society).

The Traders Point Creamery Store is open daily from 8:00 AM until 6:00 PM. In addition, the Creamery Café serves lunch Wednesdays and Thursdays, brunch Saturdays (from November to April), and dinner Fridays (from May to October.) There is a farmers' market at the Creamery on Friday evenings through the summer, and an indoor market Saturday mornings in the winter. Check the website or call for seasonal hours.

MOROCCAN CHICKPEA AND EGGPLANT STEW

Traders Point Creamery Café chef Bryan Riddle says this summer recipe was a hit on the café's lunch menu.

- 1 cup cooked chickpeas
- 1 large eggplant, diced large
- 1 large zucchini, diced large
- 1 yellow squash, diced large
- 1 large onion, diced large
- 6 cloves garlic, minced
- 2 pounds ripe tomatoes, pureed
- 1 tablespoon ground ginger
- 1 teaspoon cinnamon
- 1 teaspoon ground coriander
- 1 tablespoon ground cumin
- 1 cup Traders Point yogurt
- 12 mint leaves, chopped

Sauté all vegetables and garlic in oil over high heat until just slightly softened. Add tomato purée, spices, and chickpeas, and cook until reduced to desired consistency. Meanwhile, add chopped mint to yogurt.

Spoon into bowls and drizzle with minted yogurt. Garnish with mint leaf. Serves 4–6.

Your Neighbor's Garden

PRODUCE

> 5224 Grandview Dr., Indianapolis IN 46228 (Marion)
> 317-251-4130 • www.yourneighborsgarden.com

It should really be no surprise that Ross Faris eventually found his way back to the soil after a career at Eli Lilly. His mother was born on a northwest Indiana farm more than 100 years ago, and the farmstead remains in the family. Ross and his wife Sherry have lovingly restored the 150-year-old farmhouse, dairy barn, smokehouse, and corn crib on 100 acres of rolling farmland located 10 miles south of LaPorte. They rent the farm out as a retreat and it's the perfect setting for family reunions, corporate functions, and other types of gatherings.

In the early 1980s, when the Farises' children Anne and Greg wanted to start a front-yard lemonade stand, they consulted with their dad, and he advised them that they could probably make more money selling fruits and vegetables from the family garden. They hauled a picnic table to the roadside and set up an on-your-honor produce stand. It did not take long for word to spread, and eventually the Faris family needed to add some acreage to grow more fruits and vegetables. Fast-forward 25 years and Anne and Greg have flown from the nest, while dad is still at it. He retired from Eli Lilly in the '90s and now devotes his energies full-time to the two acres of gardens located near their home on the northwest side of Indianapolis.

Your Neighbor's Garden stays true to its name, offering fruits and vegetables that you might find, well, in your neighbor's garden—berries, tomatoes, cucumbers, peppers, and so much more. If your thumb is a shade other than green or if you don't want to work hard enough to have your own garden, it's great to have a neighbor like Faris.

The home farm stand remains on the self-serve honor system, but Faris's fruits and vegetables are now also available in places way beyond the home front. Your Neighbor's Garden is a regular fixture at the farmers' markets in Broad Ripple, Zionsville, and Irvington, and in Indianapolis at the City Market and the farmers' market at 38th and Meridian Streets. And the consumer market is just one part of the Farises' customer base. The chefs and restaurants using his fruits and vegetables make up a Who's Who of the central Indiana culinary world. Your Neighbor's Garden also partners with many of these chefs to offer several harvest diners from June through September of each year. Each occasion features a menu centered around fresh, seasonal, local foods. So much for retirement!

The home market on Grandview Drive is open Mondays through Saturdays from 9:00 AM to 6:00 PM. Look for the "Local Produce" sign near the mailbox and drive to the rear of their home. Next to the garage is a small air-conditioned store. Step inside, pick out what you want, consult the price list, and leave your payment in the metal box. It restores one's faith in humanity to know people can still do business this way.

The Apple Works

APPLES, CIDER, BAKED GOODS

CR 250 W., Trafalgar IN 46181 (Johnson)
317-878-9317 • www.apple-works.com

Rick and Sarah Brown planted their first apple tree in 1989 and harvested their first apples in 1991. Today they grow more than 50 varieties of apples, including some rare ones you won't find anywhere else in Indiana. They also offer fresh seasonal vegetables. Their country store sells lots of apple products, and the Apple Cider Donuts are not to be missed. Apple Works offers lots of activities for kids and can also provide facilities for weddings and other events. There are special events year-round; check the website for a schedule. Apple Works is open year-round from 9:00 AM to 6:00 PM on weekdays and from 9:00 AM to 7:00 PM on weekends.

Goose the Market

BUTCHER, RETAIL SHOP

2503 N. Delaware St., Indianapolis IN 46205 (Marion)
317-924-4944 • www.goosethemarket.com

Within days of its fall 2007 opening, Goose the Market had foodies near and far buzzing with anticipation. Even before the grand opening, the website teased that Goose would be a "neighborhood specialty food and wine market . . . built around the love of phenomenal food, the people who passionately produce it and the rest of us who can't wait to get our hands on it." This was no false advertising. Former chef Chris Eley and wife Mollie decided to open Goose after a move from Chicago to Indy. It was the neighborhood markets they missed the most, so they opened one, and we're all so delighted they did. Here's just a sampling of what you can find at Goose—dry-aged beef, pork, poultry, lamb, dairy, and in-season produce from Indiana farms. They also have an amazing selection of great food from beyond the Hoosier State—more meats, cheeses, dry goods, prepared foods, and wines. Goose is closed on Mondays and open Tuesdays through Fridays from 10:00 AM to 8:00 PM, Saturdays from 10:00 AM to 6:00 PM, and Sundays from 10:00 AM to 2:00 PM.

Hancock Harvest Council

PRODUCER GROUP

> Purdue University Cooperative Extension Service,
> Hancock County, 802 N. Apple St.,
> Greenfield IN 46140 (Hancock)
> 317-462-1113 • www.ces.purdue.edu/Hancock/

Residents of Hancock County who are interested in eating local have a great shortcut available to help them develop their own network of providers. The Hancock Harvest Council is a member-supported group of farmers and others dedicated to connecting local producers with local consumers. They maintain a directory of more than 20 producers in the area. The Council gets support from the Purdue Extension office and a great deal of information, including the downloadable 50-page directory, is available on the Purdue Extension website. So in Hancock County the search for local meats, produce, and all sorts of great food should begin with the Hancock Harvest Council.

Hunters Honey

HONEY, HONEY PRODUCTS

> 3440 Hancock Ridge Rd., Martinsville IN 46151 (Morgan)
> 765-537-9430 • www.huntershoneyfarm.com

Carrying on a family tradition, the Hunters are third-generation beekeepers in Indiana, managing several hundred hives throughout the state. They produce the honey itself, as well as value-added products like candles, candy, and dog treats. The Hunters operate a gift shop onsite (open from sunup to sundown, seven days a week) and enjoy giving tours of the honey farm (call ahead or visit the website to arrange one). You can also buy their products at the Bloomington City Farmers' Market, the Bloomington Winter Farmers' Market, Bloomingfoods, and many other places, including Meijer and Wild Oats. As the Hunters like to say, "We enjoy making life sweeter for our customers."

L'Explorateur

RESTAURANT

> 6523 Ferguson St., Indianapolis IN 46220 (Marion)
> 317-726-6906 • www.dinelex.com

According to chef and owner Neal Brown, exploration is all about seeking, finding, discovering, wandering, getting lost, and coming back. At his Broad Ripple restaurant, Neal is committed to using both the familiar and the unfamiliar in unexpected ways. The journey to the plate begins with farmers, artisans, fishmongers, cheese makers, mycologists, oenologists, and lots of other people who grow or make food. Many of these culinary contributors are right here in Indiana. Some of his food is so local,

in fact, that its journey to the restaurant is shorter than
that of many of his patrons.

L'Explorateur's menu can be playful, inventive, and
simple—sometimes all on the same plate. An unadulter-
ated piece of quality local pork might be accompanied
by a mind-expanding gastro-chemical gelée or foam.
The menu at L'Explorateur is seasonal and changes every
few weeks. Depending on the time of year, it may feature
products from Traders Point Creamery, Capriole Farms,
Fair Oaks Farms, Your Neighbor's Garden, Homestead
Growers, Seldom Seen Farms, Fisher Farms, Walnut
Grove Spring Water, and more.

Home Grown Indiana

TOMATO CONSOMMÉ

*Chef Neal Brown, of L'Explorateur in Indianapolis, loves
consommés for a million reasons and uses them in his restaurant whenever he wants light, French-based techniques
that are simple in preparation and complex in flavor. He says,
"One key thing to note is that consommés are unforgiving
when the quality of the ingredients is substandard. It is of
the utmost importance to use the freshest, ripest tomatoes
you can find."*

The stock

- 2 tablespoons olive oil
- 3 small carrots, coarsely chopped
- ½ sweet onion, coarsely chopped
- 2 ribs celery, chopped
- 1 6 oz. can of tomato paste
- ⅔ cup white wine
- ¼ cup white vinegar
- 2 teaspoons sugar
- 2 large sprigs thyme
- 1 bay leaf

- 1 tablespoon peppercorns
- 8 ripe tomatoes, chopped, juice reserved
- 1 tablespoon coarse salt
- 2 cups water
- 1 cup tomato juice (better yet, reserved juice from the tomatoes)
- 1 raft (recipe below)

In a medium pot, sweat the vegetables for 4–5 minutes until soft, but do not let them brown. Add the tomato paste to the pot and cook the rawness out of it for 5–6 minutes, stirring just enough that it does not burn. Add the wine and the vinegar to deglaze the pan and reduce briefly.

Add the sugar, tarragon, thyme, bay leaf, peppercorns, tomatoes, and salt, and cook 4–5 minutes, stirring occasionally. Add the tomato juice and water.

Allow the stock to come almost to a boil, but do not let it actually boil! This will take about 10 minutes. Turn the heat down and cook on very low heat for about an hour. If you cook the stock any longer, you risk losing its fresh quality.

Strain the liquid through cheesecloth or the finest mesh strainer you have. You can even use a clean kitchen towel. This is very important because this is the first in a series of clarifications for the consommé. Press the ingredients firmly into the cheesecloth to get the maximum flavor. This is not the most enjoyable process, but will be well worth your efforts. Allow the stock to cool to room temperature.

The raft

The use of a raft may be unfamiliar to you, but it is how chefs clarify their stocks, removing all impurities to leave a crystal-clear and clean-tasting broth. Chef Brown says, "This is going to look pretty horrible for a while but have no fear, it will be awesome!"

- · 5 ounces ground chicken. If your grocery does not have it, use ground turkey. You can also grind your own chicken if you have the time and local organic chickens. This is always best!
- · 5 large egg whites, with shells
- · 1 carrot, chopped
- · 1 rib celery, chopped
- · 1 tablespoon black peppercorns
- · 3 sprigs thyme

Put all ingredients into the bowl of a food processor and pulse about ten times.

Reheat the stock over low heat. Whisk the raft into the stock rather vigorously. Stir for about 6 minutes and walk away for 25 minutes.

When you return, you will find what appears to be a monster. This is perfectly normal. Allow the consommé to cook over low heat for 90 minutes. Very carefully, cut a hole the size of a coffee cup out of the middle of the raft, removing the center disc with a slotted spoon. Ladle the consommé out through the hole and into a sieve set over a bowl and lined with yet more cheesecloth. The consommé that is strained into the bowl will store nicely in an airtight container in the fridge for 3–4 days or in the freezer for several months. Makes 6 cups.

MCL Restaurant & Bakery

RESTAURANT

15 Indiana locations (See p. 151)
317-257-4525 • www.mclhomemade.com

You have to put away all the jokes about cafeteria food when it comes to MCL Cafeteria. Sure, it has jello salad and many of the comfort-food cafeteria standbys, but it also offers plenty of fresh seasonal choices. Over the last few years, MCL has worked closely with Indiana farmers and now uses fresh Hoosier produce, beginning with blueberries and asparagus in the spring and continuing all the way through to apples in the fall. Two of the Indianapolis locations, Castleton and Township Line Road, have farmers' markets in the parking lot, open during restaurant hours Mondays through Saturdays. MCL operates 21 stores in the Midwest and 15 here in Indiana, including in Anderson, Bloomington, Carmel, Muncie, Richmond, Speedway, Terre Haute, and West Lafayette, and several in Indianapolis.

Melody Acres

PRODUCE

> 1169 North SR 135, Franklin IN 46131 (Johnson)
> 317-554-9211

Randy Stout is the fourth generation to farm this 90-year-old farm in Johnson County. Farming without commercial insecticides, pesticides, or herbicides, he grows all-season vegetables: broccoli, cabbage, winter squash, onions, sweet potatoes, and pumpkins as well as sweet corn, tomatoes, peppers, and all kinds of summer squash. Melody Acres produce is available at Bloomington area restaurants (Tallent and Roots), at Bloomingfoods and Sahara Mart, and at the Bloomington Community Farmers' Market and Winter Market.

Not Just Popcorn

POPCORN

114 E. Main Cross St., Edinburgh IN 46124 (Johnson)
800-231-5689; 812-526-8488 • www.notjustpopcorn.com

Carol Buck is a popcorn magician. In the back room of her shop in downtown Edinburgh she concocts magical flavor combinations that astonish and amaze—more than 240 flavors, to be precise. The corn she starts with is local and delicious (grown down the road from the shop by Randy Weinantz), but her flavorings put a twist on the familiar snack. There is hardly a flavor she can't mix up—everything from amaretto to bubble gum, licorice, peanut butter, or watermelon. Try the dill pickle (it's surprisingly good) and the jalapeño cheddar. She's got chocolate-covered popcorn available too. All are available by mail order and in the shop.

Pickett's Autumn Gold Sorghum

SORGHUM

1061 E. 236th St., Sheridan IN 46069 (Hamilton)
317-758-4331 • www.pickettsorghum.com

Pickett's Autumn Gold Sorghum was founded in 1913 and now a third generation of Picketts operates the family business. Every fall, they harvest and manufacture the sorghum during the six weeks from the end of August to mid-October. Pickett's products are available at their facility in Sheridan and at many grocery stores in Indiana. As for the taste, it is sweet and earthy. There's nothing quite like a warm-from-the-oven biscuit with Pickett's Sorghum. Their store is open seasonally Mondays through Saturdays from 7:00 AM to 4:00 PM. Call to confirm that they're open before stopping by.

Stuckey Farm

APPLES, PRODUCE

> 19996 County Line Rd., Sheridan IN 46069 (Hamilton)
> 866-612-9030 • www.stuckeyfarm.net

Stuckey Farm has been a fixture in rural Hamilton County since 1969. It features a pick-your-own apple orchard and pumpkin patch, and vegetables are available throughout the growing season. Homemade apple cider is tasty, too. It's a great place for families, and many of the area schools make annual field trips to the farm. In the fall, there are 13 acres of pumpkins onsite and the farm market sells jellies, jams, maple syrup, and other goods. Stuckey Farm is open Mondays through Fridays from 9:00 AM to 6:00 PM and Saturdays from 9:00 AM to 5:00 PM.

Tuttle Orchards

APPLES, CIDER, PRODUCE

> 5717 N. 300 W., Greenfield IN 46140 (Hancock)
> 317-326-2278 • www.tuttleorchards.com

The Tuttles planted their first apple tree in 1928, and now they have 4,750 of them. Several generations of the family work the orchard, growing 22 different kinds of apples, making 10,000 gallons of cider each year, and offering some of the best caramel apples you'll find anywhere. Children are always welcome and there are plenty of things to keep them busy. Tuttle has both a market and a U-Pick operation, so you can be as hands-on or hands-off as you like. The Market Store is open Mondays through Wednesdays from 9:00 AM to 6:00 PM and Thursdays through Saturdays from 9:00 AM to 7:00 PM.

Viking Lamb

LAMB

> 1634 E. 1000 N., Morristown IN 46161 (Shelby)
> 765-763-6179

Terry Knudson was just 11 years old when he raised his first lamb. Today he supplies lamb to fine restaurants, high-end retailers, and directly to discriminating consumers. Viking Lamb processes nearly every week, so both fresh and frozen cuts are available. Knudson and his crew offer a wide range of cuts and some unique sausages, including a Tabasco Brat and a smoked and fully cooked "Sheep Dog." Viking Lamb can be found at Joe's Butcher Shop & Fish Market in Carmel (p. 121), Goose the Market (p. 137), and farmers' markets in Carmel (p. 152), Noblesville (p. 154), and Indianapolis, at the 38th and Meridian Streets (p. 152) and the Binford Farmers Markets (p. 152). Products are also available at the farm. Call before visiting.

Waterman's Farm Market

STRAWBERRIES, PRODUCE

> 7010 E. Raymond St., Indianapolis IN 46239 (Marion)
> 317-357-2989
>
> Greenwood Farm Market
> Highway 37, Greenwood IN 46142 (Johnson)
> 317-888-4189 • www.watermansfarmmarket.com

Although Waterman's Farm grows lots of fruits and vegetables, the farm market is especially known for strawberries. Even when strawberry season has come and gone, you can still get a strawberry fix by picking up a jar or two of Waterman's strawberry preserves or a bag of frozen berries. The Raymond Street location in Indianapolis holds an annual Fall Harvest Festival with loads of activities for the entire family. A popular feature of the festival is Tyranny, the giant pumpkin-eating dinosaur. Call or check the website for a schedule of events and hours of operation.

Wild Oats Natural Marketplace/ Whole Foods Market

GROCERY STORE

> 14598 Clay Terrace Blvd., Carmel IN 46032 (Hamilton)
> 317-569-1517
>
> 1300 E. 86th St., Indianapolis IN 46240 (Marion)
> 317-706-0900 • www.wholefoodsmarket.com

Wild Oats was the first of the national full-service natural supermarkets to hit Indiana. The Indianapolis location in Nora Plaza quickly became a one-stop shop for those interested in organic and natural foods. The Carmel location in Clay Terrace opened a few years later to an enthusiastic reception from Hamilton County shoppers. In the summer of 2007, the Wild Oats corporation announced a merger with Austin, Texas–based Whole Foods Market, and the Wild Oats stores are scheduled for remodeling and rebranding to reemerge as Whole Foods. Both Wild Oats and Whole Foods are committed to selling locally grown foods, and Indiana stores offer local produce, dairy, eggs, and other products. Moreover, many Whole Foods locations across the U.S. have farmers' markets in their parking lots during the growing season.

GOT RAW MILK?

For serious cheese makers (and eaters), the most complex flavors really only come through when the cheese is made from raw milk: milk that has not been exposed to heat in the process of pasteurization. Judy Schad of Capriole Farms (see p. 237) says, "There is layer and layer and layer of flavor—a beginning, a middle, an end, and a finish—when you use raw milk. When you pasteurize you lose a lot of flavor-producing components." There are those, too, including members of the Weston A. Price Foundation (www.westonaprice.org), who believe that the benefits of raw milk aren't limited to cheese. They argue that milk is a "living food" and that its health value is destroyed when milk is pasteurized.

Pasteurization kills bacteria in milk and is required by law for milk that is sold for human consumption or that is used for cheeses younger than 60 days. Raw milk devotees believe that the health benefits of drinking raw milk outweigh the risk, and that in any case individual consumers should be free to take the risk if they wish. Some farmers try to circumvent the pasteurization laws by selling "pet milk," not marked for human consumption, as the Swiss Connection does (see p. 168), or by selling "cow shares." A farm can sell a share in a cow to a consumer, who thus owns a share of the cow's milk as well. The farm charges for the labor of milking and caring for the cows, but is not selling unpasteurized milk. Debbie Apple of Apple Family Farm (p. 110) has been an innovator of cow-sharing. State officials issued her a cease and desist order in 2002, but she fought back and finally got a go-ahead for her cow-share program. But because drinking raw milk does present some risk, even the Apple Family Farm website answers the question "Can you tell me why I should feed my family raw milk?" with a resounding "No!" It suggests that individuals visit many websites and gather all the information they can before making a choice about what to consume.

Ironically, some local cheese makers can find themselves at odds with the raw milk advocates, even as they use raw milk in their own aged cheeses. For example, Judy Schad has long worked to protect the right of American cheese makers to make raw milk cheeses. Large-scale cheese producers who would prefer to dispense with competition from artisanal producers like Schad, and health advocates who fear that aging raw milk cheese for only 60 days isn't enough to protect consumers, would like to see the law changed to make 60-day-old raw milk cheeses illegal, and Schad is against such a ban. But she is on the anti–raw milk side of the fence when it comes to pet milk and cow sharing. She scrupulously tests her own goat milk and knows that no matter how careful a farmer is, harmful bacteria can invade a batch of milk. If even one person gets sick from drinking unregulated pet milk, the backlash could undo the modest gains won by advocates of raw milk cheese making.

So the advice of the Apple Family Farm website remains sound—educate yourself first, and then enjoy a cold and frosty glass of the milk of your choice.

EATING LOCAL WHILE DINING OUT

120 West Market Fresh Grill
(Indianapolis Hilton)
120 W. Market St., Indianapolis IN 46204 (Marion)
317-972-0600

The Barking Dog Café
115 E. 49th St., Indianapolis IN 46205 (Marion)
765-942-2233

Bijou Restaurant
111 W. Main St., Lebanon IN 46052 (Boone)
765-482-7090 • www.bijourestaurant.net

Café Patachou
4911 N. Pennsylvania St., Indianapolis IN 46205 (Marion)
317-925-2823 • www.cafepatachou.com

8691 River Crossing Blvd., Indianapolis IN 46240 (Marion)
317-815-0765

4733 126th St., Carmel IN 46033 (Hamilton)
317-569-0965

Petite Chou by Patachou
823 Westfield Blvd., Indianapolis IN 46220 (Marion)
317-259-0765

Patachou on the Park
225 W. Washington St., Indianapolis IN 46204 (Marion)
317-632-0765

Carnegie's
100 W. Main St., Greenfield IN 46149 (Hancock)
317-462-8480

Chancellor's Restaurant
850 W. Michigan St., Indianapolis IN 46202 (Marion)
317-231-5221

Circle City Bar and Grill
(Indianapolis Marriott)
350 W. Maryland St., Indianapolis IN 46225 (Marion)
317-405-6100

City Café
443 N. Pennsylvania St., Indianapolis IN 46204 (Marion)
317-833-2233

Danielli
(Canterbury Hotel)
123 S. Illinois St., Indianapolis IN 46225 (Marion)
317-634-3000

Elements
415 N. Alabama St., Indianapolis IN 46204 (Marion)
317-634-8888 • www.elementsindy.com
See p. 113

H2o Sushi
1912 Broad Ripple Ave., Indianapolis IN 46220 (Marion)
317-254-0677 • www.h2osushibar.com

Harry and Izzy's
153 S. Illinois St., Indianapolis IN 46225 (Marion)
317-635-9594 • www.harryandizzys.com

L'Explorateur
6523 Ferguson St., Indianapolis IN 46220 (Marion)
317-726-6906
See p. 139

Oakley's Bistro
1464 W. 86th St., Indianapolis IN 46260 (Marion)
317-824-1231 • www.oakleysbistro.com

The Oceanaire Seafood Room
30 S. Meridian St., Indianapolis IN 46204 (Marion)
317-955-2277 • www.theoceanaire.com

MCL Arlington
6010 E. 10th St., Indianapolis IN 46219 (Marion)
317-356-1587 • www.mclhomemade.com
See p. 142

MCL Broad Ripple
2121 E. 62nd St., Indianapolis IN 46220 (Marion)
317-253-1908
See p. 142

MCL Carmel
Merchant's Square
1390 Keystone Way Drive E., Carmel IN 46032 (Hamilton)
317-844-9217
See p. 142

MCL Castleton
5520 Castleton Corner Lane, Indianapolis IN 46250 (Marion)
317-845-5717
See p. 142

MCL Lawrence
8135 Pendleton Pike, Indianapolis IN 46226 (Marion)
317-898-5455
See p. 142

MCL Southside
3630 S. East St., Indianapolis IN 46227 (Marion)
317-783-2416
See p. 142

MCL Township Line
2370 W. 86th St., Indianapolis IN 46260 (Marion)
317-334-1875
See p. 142

MCL Washington Square
10202 E. Washington St., Rm. 200, Indianapolis IN 46229 (Marion)
317-897-6956
See p. 142

Peterson's Restaurant
7690 E. 96th St., Fishers IN 46038 (Hamilton)
317-598-8863 • www.petersonsrestaurant.com

R bistro
888 Massachusetts Ave., Indianapolis IN 46202 (Marion)
317-423-0312 • www.rbistro.com
See p. 126

St. Elmo's Steak House
127 S. Illinois St., Indianapolis IN 46225 (Marion)
317-635-0636 • www.stelmos.com

FARMERS' MARKETS

38th and Meridian Streets Farmers' Market
3808 N. Meridian St., Indianapolis IN 46208 (Marion)
May–October, Thursdays 4:00–6:30 PM

Abundant Life Church Farmers' Market
7606 E. 82nd St., Indianapolis IN 46256 (Marion)
June–September, Thursdays 4:00 to 7:00 PM

Binford Farmers' Market
6161 E. 75th St., Indianapolis IN 46240 (Marion)
June–October, Saturdays 7:30 to 11:00 AM
www.binfordfarmersmarket.com

Broad Ripple Farmers' Market
1115 Broad Ripple Ave., Indianapolis IN 46220 (Marion)
May–October, Saturdays 8:00 AM to 12 noon
www.broadripplefarmersmarket.com

Carmel Farmers' Market
1 Civic Square, Carmel IN 46032 (Hamilton)
June–September, Saturdays 8:00 to 11:30 AM
www.carmelfarmersmarket.com

Cumberland Farmers' Market
11501 E. Washington St., Cumberland IN 46229 (Marion)
May–October, Saturdays 8:00 AM to 12 noon

Danville Farmers' Market
1 Courthouse Square, Danville IN 46112 (Hendricks)
May–September, Saturdays 8:00 AM to 12 noon

Fishers Farmers' Market
11601 Municipal Dr., Fishers IN 46038 (Hamilton)
June–October, Saturdays 8:00 AM to 12 noon
www.fishersfarmersmarket.com

Franklin Farmers' Market
Franklin Cultural Arts and Recreation Center
396 Branigin Blvd., Franklin IN 46131 (Johnson)
June–September, Saturdays 8:00 to 11:00 AM

Geist Farmers' Market
8115 Oaklandon Rd., Oaklandon IN 46236 (Marion)
May–September, Thursdays 3:30 to 7:30 PM

Gem Elevator Farmers' Market
284 S. 500 W., Greenfield IN 46140 (Hancock)
June–September, Tuesdays 4:00 to 6:30 PM

Greenfield Farmers' Market
Courthouse Square
Intersection of US 40 and State Road 9
Greenfield IN 46140 (Hancock)
June–October, Wednesdays and Saturdays 8:00 AM to 12:30 PM

Greenwood Farmers' Market
Greenwood Public Library
310 S. Meridian St., Greenwood IN 46143 (Johnson)
April–October, Wednesdays (June–September) 2:30
    to 6:00 PM, Saturdays 8:00 AM to 12 noon
www.geocities.com/GreenwoodFarmersmarket

Hancock Harvest Council Farmers' Market
888 W. New Rd., Greenfield IN 46140 (Hancock)
July–October, Saturdays 4:00 to 8:00 PM

Indianapolis Farmers' Market
222 E. Market St., Indianapolis IN 46204 (Marion)
May–October, Wednesdays 10:00 AM to 1:30 PM
www.indianapoliscitymarket.com

Irvington Farmers' Market
5301 E. Saint Clair St., Indianapolis IN 46219 (Marion)
June–October, Sundays 12 noon to 2:00 PM

Noblesville Farmers' Market
395 Westfield Rd., Noblesville IN 46060 (Hamilton)
May–October, Saturdays 8:00 AM to 12 noon
www.noblesville.biz/mainstreet/fm

Plainfield Farmers' Market
210 W. Main St., Plainfield IN 46168 (Hendricks)
May–October, Wednesdays 4:00 to 7:00 PM

Shelbyville Farmers' Market
Downtown on the Square
Shelbyville IN 46176 (Shelby)
May–October, Wednesdays and Saturdays 6:00 to 11:00 AM

Thorntown Community Market
124 W. Main St., Thorntown IN 46071 (Boone)
June–September, Saturdays 8:30 AM to 1:00 PM

Traders Point Creamery Green and Winter Markets
9101 Moore Rd., Zionsville IN 46077 (Boone)
Green Market: May–October, Fridays 4:00 to 7:00 PM;
    Winter Market: November–April, Saturdays 9:00 AM to 12 noon
www.traderspointcreamery.com

Washington Township Community Park Farmers' Market
CR 575 E., Avon IN 46123 (Hendricks)
June–October, Tuesdays 5:00 to 7:30 PM

Zionsville Farmers' Market
Intersection of Hawthorne and Main Streets
290 S. Main St., Zionsville IN 46077 (Boone)
June–September, Saturdays 8:00 AM to 12 noon

WINERIES

Buck Creek Winery
11747 Indian Creek Rd. S., Indianapolis IN 46259 (Marion)
317-862-WINE (9463) • www.buckcreekwinery.com

Chateau Thomas
6291 Cambridge Way, Plainfield IN 46168 (Hendricks)
317-837-WINE (9463) • www.chateauthomas.com

Easley Winery
205 N. College Ave., Indianapolis IN 46202 (Marion)
317-636-4516 • www.easleywinery.com

Ferrin's Fruit Winery
89 1st Ave. S.W., Carmel IN 46032 (Hamilton)
317-566-WINE (9463) • www.ferrinsfruitwinery.com

Grape Inspirations Winery
1307 S. Rangline Rd., Carmel IN 46032 (Hamilton)
317-705-WINE (9463) • www.grape-inspirations.com

Mallow Run Winery
6964 W. Whiteland Rd., Bargersville IN 46106 (Johnson)
317-422-1556 • www.mallowrun.com

MICROBREWERIES & BREWPUBS

Alcatraz Brewing
49 W. Maryland St., Indianapolis IN 46204 (Marion)
317-488-1230 • www.alcatrazbrewing.com

Barley Island Brewing Company
639 Conner St., Noblesville IN 46060 (Hamilton)
317-770-5280 • www.barleyisland.tripod.com

Broad Ripple Brewpub
840 E. 65th St., Indianapolis IN 46220 (Marion)
317-253-2739 • www.broadripplebrewpub.com

Brugge Brasserie
1011a E. Westfield Blvd., Indianapolis IN 46220 (Marion)
317-255-0978 • www.bruggebrasserie.com

Oaken Barrel Brewing
50-L N. Airport Pkwy., Greenwood IN 46143 (Johnson)
317-887-2287 • www.oakenbarrel.com

Ram Brewery
140 S. Illinois St., Indianapolis IN 46225 (Marion)
317-955-9900 • www.theram.com

Rock Bottom Brewery
2801 Lake Circle Dr., Indianapolis IN 46268 (Marion)
317-471-8840 • www.rockbottom.com

Rock Bottom Brewery
10 W. Washington St., Indianapolis IN 46204 (Marion)
317-681-8180 • www.rockbottom.com

FOOD FESTIVALS

Grape Harvest Festival
Winery tours, tastings, food and wine demonstrations
Early October
Plainfield IN (Hendricks)
800-761-WINE (9463) • www.chateauthomas.com

Rib America Festival
BBQ professionals from across the US
Indianapolis IN (Marion)
Labor Day Weekend
317-249-2710 • www.ribamerica.com

Shelbyville Strawberry Festival
Shelbyville IN (Shelby)
Strawberry shortcake, ice cream, and other treats
Mid-June
317-398-9623

Strawberry Festival on Monument Circle
Indianapolis IN (Marion)
Strawberry shortcake
Mid-June
317-636-4577

Vintage Indiana
Indianapolis IN (Marion)
More than 100 wines, wine seminars, and food
Early June
800-832-WINE (9463) • www.vintageindiana.com

5

Southwest

Southwest Indiana is the smallest region in this book, covering just eleven counties, from Vigo, Clay, and Owen on the north border to Gibson, Pike, and Dubois on the south. The region is famous for its great fried chicken places (try The Chicken Place in Ireland) and old-style German food (notably Schnitzelbank in Jasper), but for locally produced foods, what mostly comes to mind in southwest Indiana is melons. The stretch of Highway 41 that runs through Knox County is a veritable "Melon Alley"—it is lined with melon farms, most of which have farm markets open during the summer months.

But melons aren't the only homegrown treat on offer in southwest Indiana, even if the folks there once considered their region the melon capital of the world. In addition to gorgeous fruit and vegetables, the region produces everything from beef and chickens to eggs and cheese, to baking powder and grits. For the most part the farms aren't large and the towns are small, but the area is well worth a visit for the friendly faces and good eating that await.

ButtonWoods at Sycamore Farm

RESTAURANT

5001 E. Poplar Dr., Terre Haute IN 47803 (Vigo)
812-877-9288 • www.thesycamorefarm.com

Suburban sprawl comes even to Terre Haute. Once a working farm of 800 acres in the middle of the countryside, Sycamore Farm is now surrounded by housing developments, its old 1860s farmhouse a graceful, if slightly forlorn, reminder of days gone by. But the farmhouse succeeds in combining modern comfort with the graciousness of the past. The house itself has been transformed into an amazingly comfortable bed and breakfast, and its parlors and porches have become the intimate dining spaces that constitute ButtonWoods at Sycamore Farm. The restaurant is open for lunch Tuesdays through Fridays and for dinner Friday nights.

The newly refurbished kitchen is under the guidance of Chef Kris Kraut, self-taught and young, but very proficient. An intuitive cook, Kraut creates his recipes and plans the menu around what local farmers have to offer. He is fiercely dedicated to cooking from scratch and determined to cut no corners. He is also, by the way, recently married to the daughter of Sycamore Farm's owner Marilyn Oehler, whom he has been dating since they were in the 7th grade!

Oehler says her restaurant is "brasserie-style farm-fresh cuisine," and that seems to put it just right. The cooking isn't fancy or fussy, but it is fresh and honest and delicious. Kraut's menu changes weekly. One summer night the first courses were chilled tomato buttermilk soup, cool and spicy, and a salad with gorgeous fresh berries, goat cheese, and pistachios in a cherry vinaigrette. Entrees were White Caps (delicate pan-fried fish cakes made from Michigan white fish) with lemon garlic aioli, yellow beans and cherry tomatoes, a Heartland Beef filet (grass-finished!) with blueberry barbeque sauce, a grilled Royer Farm leg of lamb with red and yellow pepper relish and spiced basmati rice, pineapple chipotle chicken with grilled corn and cilantro butter, and grilled squash and roasted tomatoes in a creamy wine marinara sauce over pasta. Most of the produce comes from farmer Darin Kelly, of Good Life Farms in Terre Haute (p. 174).

There are several dining rooms downstairs, including one cozy room with a fireplace for chilly evenings and a glassed-in, light-filled room with a view of the patio and gazebo. And the beauty of it is, if you plan it right, all you have to do when you are finished is toddle up the stairs to your room. Perfect!

ROASTED PORK TENDERLOIN WITH CHERRY RHUBARB CHUTNEY

Chef Kris Kraut of ButtonWoods at Sycamore Farm created this pork tenderloin recipe to make tart and spicy use of the spring bounty of rhubarb.

Chutney

- ¾ cup sugar
- ⅓ cup apple cider vinegar
- 1 tablespoon fresh ginger root, peeled and minced
- ½ teaspoon ground cinnamon
- ½ teaspoon ground cumin
- 2 cloves garlic, minced
- ½ teaspoon ground cloves
- ¼ teaspoon crushed red pepper
- 4 cups fresh rhubarb, chopped (about 1½ pounds)
- ⅔ cup red onion, chopped
- ½ cup dried tart cherries

Pork Tenderloins

- 2 pork tenderloins from Royer Farm (p. 98) or your local producer (about 1½ pounds total)
- ¼ teaspoon ground cloves
- 2 teaspoons ground cumin
- 1 tablespoon extra-virgin olive oil
- Salt and pepper to taste

To prepare the chutney, combine first eight ingredients in a large saucepan and bring to a simmer over low heat, stirring until the sugar dissolves. Add the rhubarb, onion, and cherries and increase the heat to medium high. Cook mixture until the rhubarb is tender and the mixture thickens slightly, about 10 minutes. Cool to room temperature. This may be made up to a day ahead, covered, and chilled, and brought up to room temperature before serving.

Preheat the oven to 400°. Season the tenderloins with cloves, cumin, and salt and pepper to taste. In a large skillet, heat olive oil over medium-high heat and brown on both sides, about 5 minutes. Transfer to a roasting pan and brush with 6 tablespoons of the chutney. Roast the meat until it reaches an internal temperature of 155–160°, brushing occasionally with 6 more tablespoons of chutney, about 25 minutes. Cut the tenderloins into 1-inch-thick slices and serve with the remaining chutney. Serves 4.

Fischer Farms

BEEF

Kyana IN 47505 (Dubois)
812-481-1411 • www.ffnatural.com

The tiny town of Kyana is just a blip on the map, but it has been home to the Fischer family farm for going on five generations. Today Dave Fischer, great-grandson of the Fischer who bought the farm in 1870, has converted his 700 acres of corn and soybeans to pasture for more than 300 cattle and has created a thriving beef business that supplies restaurants and stores across the southern half of the state.

Before coming back to the farm, Fischer spent 15 years as a computer software consultant. Though he had been a part-owner of the farm since 1996, his dad was running it and Dave and his wife Diana were living in Dallas and Germany. But he knew he'd be coming home one day, and since the prospect of growing corn didn't thrill him, he looked around for another way to make money off the farm.

In the conventional way that beef is raised in the United States, farmers like the Fischers breed cows and raise the calves until they are old enough to leave their moms, then send them off to feedlots to be fattened up for market. On the feedlots the young calves are generally confined and fed grain products, along with hormones to speed their growth and antibiotics to keep them from getting ill in the cramped conditions. The result is the richly marbled beef Americans have grown accustomed to eating, but meat that comes with chemical residue.

Disenchanted with his experiences with the beef brokers who came to buy his calves, Fischer reconsidered the process and decided to raise the cows entirely on his farm and process them locally. He felt that he needed to finish them on grain to get the marbling he wanted and to raise the number of cattle he wanted to sell, but he decided on an all-natural, more humane process that avoids the growth hormones and the need for antibiotics.

The Fischers welcome visitors to their farm to see the facilities and cows, and such transparency is reassuring in a time when much meat is raised and processed out of public view. The Fischers' cows live outdoors, rotated from pasture to pasture, until they are about 10 months old. Then they are brought inside, where their diet can be more controlled, and fed on an all-natural blend of grain and hay. The animals are processed nearby, at Sanders Processing Plant, and shipped out to area stores and restaurants.

Fischer Farms beef, as well as the Stanley Hall pork Fischer distributes for a nearby farmer, is available at leading restaurants in Bloomington and Indianapolis and at stores in Jasper, Evansville, Bloomington, and Indianapolis. See the website for specifics, or call to arrange a visit.

Harvest Moon Flower Farm

BERRIES, VEGETABLES, FLOWERS

3592 Harvest Moon Lane, Spencer IN 47460 (Owen)
812-829-3517 • www.harvestmoonflowerfarm.com

Linda Chapman is a farmer, and her body telegraphs her outdoor life from the moment you meet her. She is tall, lithe, and strong, with her streaky gray-blond hair pulled back from a face deeply tanned in summer and her blue eyes crinkled with laughter and sun. Though she looks born to it, a farmer is the last thing Chapman planned to become. Growing up in suburbia, she says she thought "farmers lived on some other planet"—and yet, here she is.

Thirty years after they bought a barren cow pasture out in Owen County, she and her partner, Deryl Dale, have transformed it into the lush and gorgeous Harvest Moon Flower Farm. Walking onto their property in summer is like that moment when Dorothy steps out of her black-and-white Kansas house and into a Technicolor Oz—dazzling color blazes from row after row of wildly beautiful flowers and berry bushes. That's what Chapman loves best about being a farmer: "Waking up and walking out my front door and seeing beauty all around me. . . . It's a good life," she says.

Chapman has her hands full creating beautiful floral wedding decorations (about 25 weddings per season), supplying flowers and vegetables to restaurants throughout the Bloomington area, and keeping up with farmers' markets. As if that didn't keep her busy enough, in 2005, long convinced that Bloomington needed a winter farmers' market, she decided to make one happen.

With the support of Slow Food Bloomington, Chapman began the market in the gymnasium of the Harmony School. Now under the sponsorship of the Local Growers Guild, the market gives area growers a winter outlet for their products and Bloomington consumers get year-round access to fresh, local food. The Winter Market has changed the way farming is done at Harvest Moon. Dale constructed hoop houses—greenhouse-like structures with plastic stretched over a framed space big enough to work in—that allow Chapman to keep planting and harvesting throughout the winter but which alter the cycle of her work year dramatically.

In 2006 Chapman and Dale were chosen as Slow Food Bloomington delegates to Terra Madre, an international Slow Food conference on sustainable food production in Torino, Italy. For Chapman, Terra Madre was an amazing event that reinforced her belief that the "little farmers" of the world are our global heritage and our best way of ensuring food security. She also met a new "farmer mentor" here in the United States who has helped her get better at what she loves to do. She and Dale are excited about ways to expand and enhance what they do on the farm.

Harvest Moon Farm sells its products at the Bloomington Community Farmers' Market, the Bloomington Winter Farmers' Market, the Broad Ripple Farmers' Market, and the Indianapolis City Market. Visitors are welcome to the farm on Sundays and Mondays in May from 12 noon til 5:00 PM, and on several "farm evenings" in July when everything is in bloom. See the website for details and directions.

Melon Acres

ASPARAGUS, MELONS, CUCUMBERS

> 5388 E. Gauger Rd. (on the west side of US 41)
> Oaktown IN 47561 (Knox)
> 812-745-2807 • www.melonacres.com

The machinery in Willie Wonka's chocolate factory may be pretty cool, but it has nothing on the Horall family's amazing asparagus sorter. Located in a huge warehouse on the family farm in Oaktown, just north of Vincennes, whose cavernous rooms are stacked high with green and purple asparagus, the machine processes 1,700–2,000 pounds of the vegetable per hour, sizing it and collecting it into neat one-pound bundles for human hands to gather, wrap in signature purple rubber bands, and ship off to a grocery store near you.

The machine, based on one the Horalls found in New Zealand, is amazing. Farm workers guide the asparagus spears into individual metal compartments, and the spears ride a moving belt up to a box where a digital camera takes a picture of each one, measures its length and circumference, and assigns it a value. The spears continue to roll along the assembly line until they come to a slot with other spears of their size. Then a magnet releases their compartment and they pop out into the air and fall down a chute. At the bottom, they accumulate into one-pound lots, to be bundled up by human hands. When the machine is rolling at full speed, the asparagus merrily jumping out into midair, the whole business of commercial asparagus farming looks like a lot of easy fun.

It is no such thing, of course. The Horalls—Abner, who bought the farm in 1976, his son Mike, and now his daughter Autumn—are family farmers, working their 1800-acre farm in Knox County, once known as "the melon capital of the world." In order to keep the migrant workers they employ busy throughout the season, they have expanded beyond the melons they began with. In 2007, they grew 120 acres of asparagus, 400 of cantaloupe, 400 of watermelon, a couple hundred of sweet corn, and 30 of cucumbers. This is not just market farming (though the farm has its own market in the summer months)—the farm is successful on a commercial scale, selling produce to grocery stores and restaurants all over the country.

You can order produce from the Melon Acres website, and the on-farm market is open from July 4 til after Labor Day, from 8:00 AM to 8:00 PM daily. As well as Melon Acres' own produce, it also sells choice produce from neighboring farms, novelty foods like asparagus guacamole and asparagus salsa, and local treats like jams, jellies, and honey.

Make a day trip of it, visiting the other five or six melon stands and farm markets up and down Highway 41 north of Vincennes (p. 176), and, if it's a weekend, stopping for a home-cooked meal at McKinley Orchards, just across the street, where Melon Acres produce is likely to be on the menu (see the restaurant profile on p. 175).

Swiss Connection

CHEESE, DAIRY

1363 E. 550 S., Clay City IN 47841 (Clay)
812-939-2813 • www.swissconnectioncheese.com

For a man whose two main food groups are meat and cheese, Alan Yegerlehner seems unusually happy to talk about his cholesterol levels: They happen to be perfect. Good genes? Just born under a lucky food star? In this world of shifting nutritional certainties, isn't the one thing we know that a diet high in animal fats is bad for us?

Apparently not. Yegerlehner, in company with a growing number of other grass-fed beef enthusiasts, believes that what counts in cholesterol is not what we eat but what our animals eat. And what ruminants such as cows should eat, according to these folks, is the food that they are especially equipped to digest: grass and legumes, not the grain that is far more often fed to them. (See "Why Grass-Fed Beef?" on p. 251.)

The Yegerlehners (Alan, wife Mary, and daughter Kate) have only been in the cheese business since the summer of 2000. Alan had long been interested in finding a food that they could make on the farm, which had been in their family since the original Jegerlehners, newly arrived from Switzerland, bought it in 1860. A visit back to Switzerland in 1996 gave him the answer. Every village they visited made its own type of cheese, and Alan, whose thinking had already been moving cheeseward, was fascinated.

Even before the trip, the Yegerlehners had been switching their cows' feed from grain to pasture. Making cheese from the milk of those cows offered the perfect way to close the circle, to produce a complete food from the animals that grazed on the land. Farmstead cheese production could make their family farm a model of sustainable agriculture.

They came back from Switzerland fired up. A former cheese maker sold all his equipment to Alan and gave him lessons on how to use it. The Yegerlehners are committed to the philosophy of producing quality organic food, and Alan is passionate about the health dividend that comes from eating grass-fed cattle products.

The Yegerlehners sell their cheeses, as well as ice cream and meat, at the Bloomington Farmers' Market, the Traders Point Green Market, the Geist Farmers' Market, and the Terre Haute Farmers' Market. You can also find their cheeses at many restaurants and stores in central Indiana (see their website for a full listing). They welcome visitors to their onsite farm market as well, which is open April through December Mondays to Fridays from 9:00 AM to 5:00 PM and Saturdays from 9:00 AM to 4:00 PM, and January to March Saturdays from 9:00 AM to 4:00 PM. Call ahead to arrange a visit during cheese-making hours.

Walnut Grove Spring Water Persimmon Valley Farm

SPRING WATER, PERSIMMONS

Bloomfield IN 47424 (Greene)
877-947-9420 (toll free)
812-384-9395 • www.walnutgrovespring.com

Duane Smith was seeing things again. Where others saw scrubby trees, sticker bushes, and a dilapidated, rundown dairy operation, he sketched in rolling hills, a lovely home, and fields of the persimmon trees that he was hankering to grow. In 1997 Smith (who in his day job is an insurance underwriter) bought his first 40 acres, the start of the spectacularly beautiful 188-acre, 4,000-tree Persimmon Valley Farm he owns in Greene County.

That vision came in handy again a year or two later, when Smith was setting posts for a pole barn on the property and needed some water to mix the cement. Recalling that he'd seen a ditch with water in it nearby, he went to fetch some and found it icy and clear, flowing across a sandy bottom. Where some of us might have seen just a way to mix cement, or perhaps a cold drink on a hot day, he saw something else. Today Kroger buys about 12,000–18,000 gallons of the pure spring water daily, filling shiny 6,000-gallon tankers five days a week, and boutique bottles of Walnut Grove Spring Water, hand-processed in Smith's plant, are being served in fine restaurants across the country.

The persimmon farm and spring water facility had its genesis in Smith's love for his grandmother's persimmon pudding, made with the fruit from a tree in her yard. He thought it would be great to start a farm, get a persimmon orchard planted, and have it ready as a retirement business. The only hitch is that, while persimmons grow wild in the American south and thrive in Indiana, they don't take kindly to domestication and are not an easy commercial proposition.

That didn't stop Smith, who is convinced that the persimmon is the kiwi of tomorrow: "the next big fruit." He imagines a world where persimmon is a favorite ice cream flavor (percinnamon, anyone?), where "persimmon" is a color on one of Martha Stewart's paint chips, and where the rolling hills of southern Indiana become a Napa Valley of persimmon farms. To help make it happen he consulted persimmon experts and planted all 4,000 trees by hand, and the orchard will soon be bearing fruit regularly.

Finding the water was just a bonus. It is one of the very few springs left in Indiana that fertilizers, pesticides, and other chemical runoff haven't rendered unfit for consumption, and Smith is determined to take care of it. That means refusing to overpump a source that runs below ground at speeds faster than 1000 gallons per minute, shutting the pump off at night, and turning down lucrative offers from companies like Nestlé that have wanted to buy him out.

Smith's current goal is to develop the boutique bottled water business, a business that will exist almost solely thorough ecommerce. He figures he can't compete with the Nestlés and Cokes of the world, and he doesn't want to, so he is staying focused on what he can do well—offering white-tablecloth restaurants and individuals what he calls "the best-tasting water there is." His production process relies on human hands as well as on machines, and he will be hiring handicapped workers from Stonebelt to do some of the bottling tasks. "It's win/win capitalism," he explains. "We help people out and they help us out."

Water can be ordered from Walnut Grove Spring's website, and visits can be arranged by calling the office.

WILD AMERICAN PERSIMMON PUDDING

Duane Smith has fond memories of eating this pudding as a child and still craves the "sticky corners" that form as the pudding bakes.

- · 2 cups wild American persimmon pulp
- · 2 cups white sugar
- · 2 eggs, beaten
- · 1 cup whole milk
- · 1 cup buttermilk

- ¼ cup melted butter
- 1¾ cups flour
- 1 teaspoon baking soda
- 1 teaspoon baking powder

Preheat oven to 350˚. Combine persimmon pulp, eggs, milk, and buttermilk in a bowl and mix well. Mix flour, baking soda, and baking powder in another bowl. Now combine contents of both bowls. Pour into a 13 × 9 × 3" ungreased baking pan and bake 1 hour. Remove and let cool for approximately 10 minutes. Serve in shallow bowls with milk, ice cream, whipping cream, or all three. Serves 9.

To get the "sticky corners" Smith loves, stir the pudding three times, at 20-minute intervals, while it bakes, and let it cool for 15 minutes.

The Big Peach Market

PRODUCE, PRESERVED FOODS, PIES

7738 N. Old 41, Bruceville IN 47516 (Knox)
812-324-2548

The Big Peach Market is famous for, well, its big peach—a landmark that has drawn visitors to this stretch of Highway 41 since the 1950s. Today the market is owned by Bruce and Margo Donnar. Margo is sister to Sandy McKinley of McKinley Orchards, p. 175, and Barbara Lamb of Lamb's Melon Market, p. 176, making this stretch of US 41 a family affair. The Donnars sell produce from their own farm ("It's easier to tell you what we don't grow than what we do," says Margo), as well as Sandy McKinley's amazing pies and all kinds of jams, jellies, canned vegetables, pickles, popcorn, sorghum, and other goodies. Margo also sews, and the shop carries her quilts and hot pads. The Big Peach opens in mid-May with strawberry season and closes after the pumpkins and apples sell out around Halloween. Hours are from 9:00 AM to 6:00 PM, and from 7:00 AM to 7:00 PM in July and August.

Clabber Girl

BAKING PRODUCTS

> 900 Wabash Ave., Terre Haute IN 47807 (Vigo)
> 812-478-7223 • www.clabbergirl.com

Clabber Girl has been a household name for more than 150 years, with baking powder as the cornerstone of the company's product line. The Clabber Girl Museum in Terre Haute tells both the Clabber Girl story and the story of a bygone era in Indiana's history. Antonia's Country Store offers Clabber Girl baking products and lots of other Indiana products. The adjacent Clabber Girl Bake Shop serves breakfast and lunch, and the menu features many items prepared with Clabber Girl products. The museum is open Mondays through Fridays from 10:00 AM until 6:00 PM and Saturdays from 9:00 AM until 3:00 PM.

Corn Flour Producers

CORNMEAL

> RR2, Box 376, Hwy. 67, Worthington IN 47471 (Greene)
> 812-875-3113 • 866-55-FLOUR (866-553-5687)
> www.cfpmasa.com

Buying corn from more than a dozen southern Indiana farmers in Greene, Daviess, Sullivan, and Knox counties, Corn Flour Producers uses facilities installed in an old meat-processing plant in Greene County to mill white and yellow corn for tortilla making. It sells mostly to tortilla factories in Atlanta and New York, but does sell locally in Evansville. The company does not conduct regularly scheduled tours of the production facility, but will arrange them for interested parties.

Dewig Meats

BEEF, PORK, POULTRY

100 E. Maple St., Haubstadt IN 47639 (Gibson)
812-768-6208 • www.dewigmeats.com

The Dewig family (pronounced Day-wig), which has been in the meatpacking and butchering business for nearly a century, is famous for its bratwurst (extolled in the March 2002 issue of *Saveur* magazine), sausages, luncheon loafs, and freezer pork and beef. Sourcing much of their meat locally, the Dewigs are a farmer-friendly operation (in 1999 the *Wall Street Journal* noted the family's reluctance to take advantage of the glut on the pork market) with an eye to the customer as well—they stock a 60-foot counter with fresh and frozen meats and meat products. Their retail market in Haubstadt is open Mondays to Fridays from 7:00 AM til 5:00 PM.

Good Life Farms

VEGETABLES, FRUIT

Terre Haute IN 47803 (Vigo)
765-346-9992 • www.goodlifefarms.com

Darin Kelly farms a couple of acres in Vigo County, growing more than 30 kinds of fruits and vegetables. He works closely with Chef Kris Kraut at ButtonWoods at

Sycamore Farm to provide the restaurant with a variety of fresh vegetables for as long as the growing season can be made to last. Kelly also sells at the Plainfield Farmers' Market and at the Clabber Girl Market in Terre Haute.

Long Elk Farm

ELK

> RR 3, Box 406, Bloomfield IN 47424 (Greene)
> 812-863-7167 • www.indianaelkmeat.com

From the elk burgers at Nick's English Hut (p. 215) to cocoa-dusted elk steaks at Restaurant Tallent (p. 200), Long Elk Farm products are providing an unusual touch to the menus of central Indiana restaurants. With a herd 40 strong on their Greene County farm (and hopes of increasing it to 150), Duane and Becky Long sell all kinds of elk steaks, roasts, sausages, burgers, and jerky, as well as other elk products like the hides, antlers, and teeth. Their farm store is open on weekdays between 6:00 and 9:00 PM, and they sell at the Bloomington Farmers' Market and at Sahara Mart in Bloomington. Look for Long Elk Farm products also at Back in Time Natural Foods and John's Famous Stews in Indianapolis.

McKinley Orchards

PRODUCE, RESTAURANT

> 14469 N. Old 41, Oaktown IN 47561 (Knox)
> 812-745-4175

The McKinley family farm, off Highway 41, provides the bounty for a summer market stand but also for a cozy, 130-seat year-round restaurant that is as close as you can get to eating dinner at Grandma's house without an actual genetic link. The restaurant, run by Sandy and Hugh McKinley with the able assistance of grandson Austin, is open Fridays and Saturdays, starting at 4:30 Knox County time (5:30 Eastern Time). It offers a small buffet with various salads, spiced apples, fried chicken, and ham rolls (two things the restaurant is famous for), as well as sliced ham, pot roast, perfect mashed potatoes, gravy, seasonal local vegetables, and fabulous sweet and yeasty rolls. To wash it all down, there are bottomless pitchers of iced tea (sweet or unsweetened) and lemonade. And do not miss the fabulous pies, made from local fruit, for dessert!

Melon Markets on Highway 41

MELONS, FRESH PRODUCE

> Various road stands
> Highway 41, north of Vincennes
> Vincennes IN 47591 (Knox)

If you are in the mood for melons on a hot summer day, head south from Terre Haute on Highway 41. As you approach Vincennes, around the tiny town of Oaktown, the melon markets start to appear on the side of the road (Knox County claims to produce more than 70 percent of Indiana and Illinois melons).

Melon Acres is the largest operation (see p. 166). Three of the other farm markets are owned individually by three sisters (Barbara Lamb, Sandy McKinley, and Margo Donnar) and their husbands. Barbara and Larry Lamb run Lamb's Melon Market, open seasonally at 1182 W. County Rd. 1100 S. in Oaktown. McKinley Orchards has a restaurant that is worth seeking out (see p. 175), and the Donnars' Big Peach Market, the biggest one (and the hardest to miss), has a giant peach to guide you in (see

p. 172). The other produce markets deserve a stop too—
you can almost make a day of it. Most market stands on
Highway 41 open around July 4 and stay open through
Labor Day. Hours vary.

Olde Lane Orchard

FRUIT, BAKED GOODS

> 13381 E. 1325 N., Odon IN 47562 (Daviess)
> 812-636-4480

Chester and Janice Lehman have run this family business
in Davies County with the help of their children since
2002. In addition to the orchard, they have a homemade
greenhouse, a one-acre vegetable garden, and a bakery that helps keep them busy during the non-growing
months. They sell their products at farmers' markets in
Bloomington, winter and summer. Regular customers
can buy from their home.

Other Side of the Fence Farm

BEEF, CHICKEN, EGGS

> 2180 S. 650 W., Huntingburg IN 47542 (Dubois)
> 812-630-1985

Four generations and 100 years of family farming stand
behind the beef and poultry at Other Side of the Fence
Farm. Marty and Lisa Whitsitt raise 70 cows on 250 acres
in Dubois County on a rotational grazing system without
hormones, antibiotics, or other medications. They sell the
beef by the whole, half, or quarter, and also sell chickens
and eggs. Sales are direct, and customers must call ahead
to order as stocks are not kept on hand.

Rhodes Family Farm

CHICKEN, EGGS, DUCK EGGS, BEEF, PORK

Rt. 1, Box 96, Newberry IN 47449 (Greene)
812-659-2988 • 812-384-7409 (cell)

The Rhodes family (Luke, Arlene, and their six sons and one daughter) work a 100-acre farm in Greene County. They raise dairy cows for cow sharing (the milk is certified organic), grass-fed beef cattle, pastured chicken, ducks, and pork. Their 1000 chickens are pastured on the fields the cows have recently grazed, transported by two old busses the Rhodeses have tailored for the purpose. Pork is sold by the half and the whole, and beef by the cut or as ground meat. Chickens, which they process onsite, are available at the farm, and milk from the cow share program can be picked up there weekly. (See "Got Raw Milk?" on p. 148.) Call ahead to see what is available. The Rhodeses sell their eggs at the Bloomington Community Farmers' Market on Saturday mornings and at Sahara Mart and Bloomingfoods in Bloomington.

Tucker Farms Produce

PRODUCE

5638 South SR 59, Clay City IN 47841 (Clay)
812-201-8796 • 812-939-0182

Tucker Farms Produce grows sweet corn, tomatoes, strawberries, raspberries, and green beans. Much of the crop is U-Pick, but it is also sold at the onsite farm market. The market opens when the strawberries ripen in May and runs through mid-August. It is open from 9:00 AM til 6:00 PM, or until they sell out.

Wibs Stone Ground Grain

FLOUR, POLENTA, GRAIN

116 45 E. 1625 N., Odon IN 476562 (Daviess)
812-636-8066

Wibs Stone Ground Grain is a second-generation family farm that grows open-pollinated, non–genetically modified corn and wheat and processes them into flour and meal. Polenta made with Wibs rich yellow cornmeal is a southern Indiana treat. Wibs grits can be found in fine area restaurants like Restaurant Tallent (p. 200) and FARMbloomington (p. 192). Call the farm to purchase, or visit Bloomington's Saturday Farmers' Market, where the tantalizing smell of fresh, hot kettle corn will lead you right to the family's booth.

White Violet Center for Eco-Justice

PRODUCE

Sisters of Providence, 1 Sisters of Providence
Saint Mary of the Woods IN 47876 (Vigo)
812-535-2930 • www.spsmw.org

The Sisters of Providence are a congregation of Catholic women religious committed to working for positive change in the world. Their White Violet Center for Eco-Justice is a multifaceted enterprise, extending their ministry to the realm of sustainable agriculture on both a local and a global scale. Among the Center's food-producing projects are 343 acres of organic farmland producing corn and soy, an organic kitchen and market garden, and a variety of fruit orchards. Heirloom vegetables and other organic, biodynamic produce are sold at the Sisters of Providence Market on Wednesdays from May through September and at the Terre Haute Farmers' Market. Tours are available.

WHAT IS A CSA?

Throughout this book, among the details about where and how to buy farm products, you will see the acronym CSA. Far less mysterious than they sound, these letters stand for "community-supported agriculture," a simple arrangement between farmers and consumers under which people pay a lump sum to the farmers before the start of the growing season, and in return receive freshly harvested produce weekly from spring through fall.

The joy of joining a CSA is in opening that weekly box, not knowing for sure what it will contain, and finding treasure troves of fresh, crisp produce. When we fill our basket at market, we tend to choose things we already know and love, but in a CSA, someone does the choosing for us, often surprising us and expanding our culinary horizons. Much of what the farmers grow is, of course, familiar, but some of it might also be more unusual. Many CSAs provide you with recipes for using up that unexpected bounty of Swiss chard or zucchini, or that unfamiliar tatsoi.

CSAs are intended to make local, small-scale agriculture a viable enterprise. With CSAs, everyone wins. Members get their food at competitive prices, keep their money in the community, and support small local farms. They also have the opportunity to be part of the growing process—to have input on the crops that are planted and to walk the rows of growing plants. The farmers, in turn, have their production expenses guaranteed, eliminate waste, and don't have to spend valuable time marketing their produce. If they are lucky they may even gain a few eager souls to help transplant seedlings or harvest the beans.

It's true that if there's a drought or the locusts come, the weekly boxes may suffer. But farming is always a risky business, and we all share those risks anyway, ether by paying higher food prices or by paying taxes to subsidize colossal agribusinesses. CSAs let us share in the enterprise of feeding ourselves in more soul-satisfying and community-building ways.

The CSA idea originally came to the U.S. from Europe via Japan, where a group of women, fighting to stave off growing food imports and save local farms, came up with a strategy called teikei, translated roughly as "putting the farmer's face on food." While the details of CSAs may vary (some involve just one vegetable farm, for instance, while others are essentially cooperative arrangements among farmers, providing customers with a mix of produce, eggs, and dairy products), what they have in common is giving all of us, in this corporate agricultural age, a chance to put the farmers' faces back on our food.

You can read about some Indiana CSAs on pp. 30, 38, 63, 64, 117, 209, and 210.

EATING LOCAL WHILE DINING OUT

ButtonWoods at Sycamore Farm
5001 E. Poplar Dr., Terre Haute IN 47803 (Vigo)
812-877-9288 • www.thesycamorefarm.com
See p. 160

McKinley Orchards Restaurant
14469 N. Old 41, Oaktown IN 47561 (Knox)
812-745-4175
See p. 175

MCL Meadows
Intersection of 25th and Poplar Streets
3 Meadows Lane, Terre Haute IN 47803 (Vigo)
812-232-5548 • www.mclhomemade.com
See p. 142

FARMERS' MARKETS

Huntingburg Farmers' Market
Downtown between 3rd and 4th Streets
Huntingburg IN 47542 (Dubois)
July–September, Saturdays 7:00 AM to 12 noon

Jasper Farmers' Market
201 Mill St., Jasper IN 47546 (Dubois)
July–October, Saturdays 7:00 AM to 12 noon

Pike County Farmers' Market
115 Pike Ave., Petersburg IN 47567 (Pike)
June–October, Saturdays 8:30 to 11:30 AM

St. Mary of the Woods Farmers' Market
White Violet Center for Eco-Justice, 1 Sisters of Providence
Saint Mary of the Woods IN 47876 (Vigo)
Wednesdays 3:00 to 5:00 PM, in season
www.spsmw.org
See p. 174

Terre Haute Farmers' Market
Intersection of 9th and Cherry Streets
Terre Haute IN 47807 (Vigo)
June–October, Saturdays 8:00 AM to 12 noon

Vincennes Farmers' Market
112 N. 2nd St., Vincennes IN 47591 (Knox)
June–October, Wednesdays and Saturdays 7:00 AM
    to 12 noon, Thursdays 5:00 to 7:00 PM

WINERIES

Kapp Winery
8716 West SR 56, Jasper IN 47546 (Dubois)
812-482-6115

Windy Knoll Winery
845 Atkinson Rd., Vincennes IN 47591 (Knox)
812-726-1600 • www.windyknollwinery.com

MICROBREWERIES & BREWPUBS

Terre Haute Brewing
401 S. 9th St., Terre Haute IN 47807 (Vigo)
812-234-2800 • www.cvbeer.com

FESTIVALS

Catfish Festival
Catfish sandwiches and catfish dinners
Petersburg IN (Pike)
Early September
812-354-8155 • www.pikecountyin.org

Cory Apple Festival
Apples, hog roast, and fish fry
Cory IN (Clay)
Mid-September
812-864-2229

Fontanet Bean Dinner Festival
Bean dinner and other foods
Fontanet IN (Vigo)
Late August
812-877-1937

International Chili Society Indiana Cook-Off
Chili cook-off and tastings
Vincennes IN (Knox)
Mid-September
812-886-0400 • www.vincennescvb.org

Oakland City Sweet Corn Festival
Indiana sweet corn, fish fry, and other foods
Oakland City (Gibson)
Late July/Early August
888-390-5825

Owen County Apple Butter Festival
Apple butter and other apple favorites
Spencer IN (Owen)
Mid-September
812-886-0400 • www.vincennescvb.org

Popcorn Festival of Clay County
*Free popcorn for everyone, popcorn-eating contest,
     and tribute to native Orville Redenbacher*
Brazil IN (Clay)
1st of October
812-448-2307 • www.popcornfest.net

Shoal's Catfish Festival
Catfish dinners and fishing contest
Shoals IN (Martin)
Early June
812-247-2828

Sullivan Rotary Corn Festival
Corn-eating contest and plenty of food
Sullivan IN (Sullivan)
Early September
800-264-6356 • www.sctb.net

Watermelon Festival
Watermelon eating and watermelon contests
Vincennes IN (Knox)
Mid-August
812-882-6440

6

Rush Fayette Union

Franklin

Decatur

Bartholomew

Brown

Monroe **SOUTHEAST &**

SOUTH CENTRAL Ripley Dearborn

Jennings

Jackson

Lawrence

Scott

Orange Washington

Southeast & South Central

The region of southeast and south central Indiana covers the counties east of (and including) Monroe, Lawrence, and Orange, except for those bordering the Ohio River. Many of these counties are hilly and rocky with limestone—not good land for large commercial farms. Still, the westernmost part of the region is abuzz with food energy, thanks largely to the presence of Bloomington. The city is home to the largest producer-only farmers' market in the state, and its thriving Slow Food movement was instrumental in starting a winter farmers' market as well. An active Local Growers Guild now runs the winter market and promotes local producers in the region. Additionally, the anthropology department of Indiana University Bloomington offers one of the nation's first Ph.D. programs in food studies. With a host of independently owned restaurants and grocery stores (both of which sell and serve increasing amounts of locally grown food), Bloomington is a happening food town.

But that is not to say that the rest of the region is sleeping. Food energy is heating up in Orange County too, where there is a flourishing farmers' market and the Lost River Community Food Co-op has just opened its market and deli in Paoli, and the farmers of Ripley County have formed a Food and Growers Association that sponsors a number of local food initiatives, including a 10-farm CSA in the eastern part of the state. Seekers of local foods will have plenty to discover in this exciting region of Indiana.

Bloomington Community Farmers' Market

MARKET

Showers Commons
401 N. Morton St., Bloomington IN (Monroe)
812-349-3738 • www.bloomington.in.gov/parks

At 8:30 on a sultry July Saturday morning, the Bloomington Community Farmers' Market hums with energy and good spirits. Eager to beat the heat, Bloomingtonians are cheerful market-goers even at that early hour. They wander the aisles, weighing fat purple eggplants in their hands, choosing the reddest tomatoes, trading gossip with friends, listening to the music and the chatter. Colors are intense and smells enticing, and stomachs begin to growl, teased with savory samples of pungent cheeses, sips of cold, thick yogurt, and the seductive crunch of a just-cooked green bean.

From April through November, the Bloomington Community Farmers' Market is a moving kaleidoscope of ripe color and freshly harvested food. It is the largest producer-only market in the state; everything sold here is grown or raised by the vendor. An average of 90 vendors assemble weekly from May through October (a smaller number come during the cooler spring and fall months), to sell cheeses, milk, fresh produce, beef, lamb, pork, eggs, and plants to about 4,000 customers every Saturday morning. For those too hungry to wait til they get home for lunch, there are Loveland Farms grilled brats and sausages, plump and zesty on a bun with onions and peppers (see p. 213), or fat, spicy tamales made by Harvest Lodge (p. 211), or sweet and salty kettle corn, freshly popped by the folks at Wibs Stone Ground Grain (p. 179).

In the 1970s, the idea of a market that would allow farmers to sell directly to the public was a novelty in Indiana, and like so many '70s ideas, it was controversial. Members of Bloomington's Parks and Recreation Board feared that the proposed location, 3rd Street Park, would become a "quagmire," and that allowing the park to be used for commercial purposes would set Bloomington on that old slippery slope, opening the door to "too many other things." They turned the proposal down.

Undaunted, market supporters kept pushing the idea and eventually, with the mayor's backing, Parks and Rec reversed its stand. "Farmer's Market Debut Big Success" read the *Bloomington Herald-Telephone* headline on July 27, 1975. Twenty-three farmers brought produce to that first market, and most sold out quickly. No one knew what to expect, or how much produce to bring. One woman sold her two bushels of cucumbers and potatoes, her dozen ears of corn, and her single cabbage in half an hour. It took a little longer for a young boy to sell his 450 pounds of potatoes, but they too were gone by the market's close.

More than 30 years on, all sorts of things have changed at the market. It has moved, for one thing, from 3rd Street Park to Courthouse Square in 1982, to the parking lot at Sixth and Lincoln in 1984, and finally to its current location in Showers Common in 1998. Its season and its hours have expanded, and the winter market now fills in during the colder months. What hasn't changed is the commitment of the Bloomington community to providing a place where area farmers and consumers can come together over the serious and joyful business of keeping a community well fed.

The Bloomington Community Farmers' Market is open Saturdays from 8:00 AM to 1:00 PM, April–September; from 9:00 AM to 1:00 PM, October–November; and from 10:00 AM to 3:00 PM on the Saturday after Thanksgiving. It is also open Tuesdays from 3:00 to 6:00 PM, June–September.

The Chilewoman

CHILES

1704 S. Weimer Rd., Bloomington IN 47403 (Monroe)
812-339-8321 • www.thechilewoman.com

It comes on you like a tropical fever. Waves of dampness bead your brow, your heart races, your lips tingle and glow. A little like love, a little like sex—and there are some who claim it is better than either—what you have here is the authentic slow burn of the chile pepper.

The Indiana expert on all things chile is a person known to both shoppers at the Bloomington Community Farmers' Market and mail-order aficionados nationwide as the Chilewoman—or, if you must have it, Susan Welsand. If you go to the Bloomington market, you've surely seen Welsand. She has long dark wavy hair and she is the only one there wearing clothes patterned with chile peppers. You'll find her standing in front of her red Chile Wagon, which is also adorned with peppers—spiky red ristras, potted plants with glowing fruits hanging heavy in their leaves like tiny Christmas ornaments, baskets filled with peppers of all sizes, shapes, and heat levels.

She's been at this chile business since the mid-1980s. Having grown up in a meat-and-potatoes household, she was fascinated with the exotic possibilities that chile growing offered. Frustrated with the limited options available locally, she started growing chiles from seeds herself.

Today she grows about 1,100 varieties, trading the seeds of open-pollinated chiles with growers around the world to help preserve endangered varieties, and shipping her own plants around the country. She is always eager to pick up new types to grow (and she takes requests), but she can't bear to give up the ones she's tried and loved (that would be all of them, to date), so the list of her chiles keeps getting longer and longer.

Susan has been selling her plants and chiles at the Bloomington market for many years, but in 1997 she began a mail-order business, and with her move onto the Internet, her sales have exploded. She ships to every state except Hawaii and to both Canada and Mexico, filing endless forms to meet the requirements for organic farming and interstate shipping.

The downside to the business is that the more successful it becomes, the more paperwork there is to do and the less time she has to spend in the garden. With a degree in journalism and art history, she has had plenty of opportunities to take a desk job, and she's turned them all down. Her greatest pleasure is still opening the greenhouse doors to see the endless rows of green plants and breathing the great earthy smell, heady with the spicy aroma of the chiles.

Susan welcomes visitors to her farm. She and her partner Terry Morgan are putting together a visitor's center and toying with the idea of building a chile market onsite to sell chile-related items and local products. It's a work in progress, she says. Plan to visit the farm, but call ahead to be sure it's a good day.

FARMbloomington

RESTAURANT, RETAIL SHOP

The Oddfellows Building
108 E. Kirkwood Ave., Bloomington IN 47408 (Monroe)
812-323-0002 • 877-440-FARM (3276)
www.farm-bloomington.com

After more than 20 years spent traveling the world and cooking in other people's restaurants, Daniel Orr came home to Indiana to open his own. The result is FARM-bloomington, Orr's bright and airy restaurant and market in the old Oddfellows Building, off Bloomington's downtown square. FARM hearkens back to the Columbus native's childhood and the Orr family farm in Princeton, Indiana.

An eclectic mix of farm memorabilia and souvenirs of the departed fraternal order for which the building is named, the décor at FARM is comfortable and relaxed, with a provocative edge. The farm motif is dominant: hangings made from old family quilts screen the dining room, images of rural life play out on the flat-screen TV over the bar, paintings done on old seed bags cover a wall, a red "silo" provides a secluded venue for dining, and the cozy downstairs saloon (specializing in artisanal beers and bourbons) is called The Root Cellar. But there are haunting reminders of the departed Oddfellows too—ceremonial masks on the wall stare blindly into the past, and metal grills and wooden panels salvaged from the original building evoke a less bucolic space.

The chief link between FARMbloomington and actual farms is not the décor, of course, but the food. Orr sources much of his food locally. From FARMmarket up front, with its selection of local meats, cheeses, and produce, as well as its seasonally changing array of salads and sandwiches, to the tapas menu at FARMbar, to the dining room of FARMrestaurant, local foods are key.

But while the ingredients of Orr's cooking may come from the farm, the recipes definitely do not. Orr's cooking style is his own. The flavors are bold, but his cooking is light. He sees his extensive travels as a key influence and asset in his cooking, letting what he's learned from cooking around the world play out on the local palate of fresh ingredients and flavors. It's food that is at once exotic and familiar.

For instance, local free-range chicken is cooked with Chinese black vinegar and sweet chili paste. Pork ribs from Fiedler Farms are slow-cooked in a rich chocolate-accented sauce with Asian overtones. Local butternut squash pairs with bananas for a sultry bisque that reflects the years Orr spent in Anguilla. Pizzas with stone-ground multigrain crusts share the menu with tropical preparations of raw fish. Seemingly disparate parts come together on Orr's plates to join into a new and happy whole.

Orr likes to say that anyone can make food taste good if he or she throws enough butter and cream at it, but the real cook's challenge is to let food taste good on its own terms. Cooking is 90 percent shopping for great ingredients and 10 percent not screwing those ingredients up. Of course, if you do screw them up, he says wryly, be sure to throw lots of butter and cream at them. Satisfied customers will have no need for extra butter and cream when they dine at FARMbloomington.

FARMbloomington is open seven days a week. Lunch is served Tuesdays through Fridays from 11:00 AM to 2:30 PM; brunch is Saturdays and Sundays from 10:00 AM to 3:00 PM; and dinner is served Tuesdays through Thursdays from 5:00 to 10:00 PM, Fridays and Saturdays from 5:00 to 11:00 PM. The restaurant is closed Sunday evenings and Mondays. The Root Cellar is open and offers live music Thursdays through Saturdays from 7:00 PM until the restaurant closes. There's a $5.00 cover charge, which is waived if you are eating in the restaurant.

BUTTERNUT AND BANANA BISQUE

Chef Daniel Orr of FARMbloomington loves this soup either hot or cold. Make it even more delicious by adding some shrimp or crabmeat or some chopped pistachio nuts.

- ¼ cup olive oil
- 2 Spanish onions, coarsely chopped
- 4 shallots, coarsely chopped
- 4 cloves garlic, minced
- 1 tablespoon fresh ginger, peeled and minced
- 1 butternut squash, peeled, seeded, and roughly chopped (or similar amount of other hard squash or pumpkin)
- 1 ripe banana
- 1 green apple, peeled, cored, and roughly chopped
- 1 hot cherry pepper (available in Caribbean markets)
- 4 cups water (or light vegetable or chicken stock)
- 1 tablespoon kosher salt
- 1 tablespoon Orr's Anguillan Jerk Spice Rub (available at FARMmarket) or another jerk spice mix
- 1 can coconut milk (optional)
- Juice of 1 lime
- Salt and pepper to taste

Heat a heavy-bottomed stainless steel pan over medium-high heat. Drizzle in the olive oil and add onions, shallots, garlic, and ginger. Reduce heat and sweat the vegetables (cooking until tender but without coloring them).

Add remaining ingredients, except the lime, salt, and pepper, to the pot. Return heat to high and bring to a boil, stirring often. Reduce heat and simmer until squash is tender. Add coconut milk if desired.

Remove cherry pepper (unless you like it spicier) and purée until very smooth. Thin as needed with additional stock or water. Season to taste with lime, salt, and pepper. Serves 6.

Heartland Family Farm

PRODUCE, EGGS

Teresa Birtles, Bedford IN (Lawrence)
812-797-6274

The farmers at Heartland Family Farm work long days and often nights as well to grow the bounty that they haul up to Bloomington several times a week in season. They have restaurants to supply—places like Restaurant Tallent, FARMbloomington, Trulli Flatbread, Nick's English Hut, and the Limestone Grille—as well as boxes to fill for subscribers to the Core Farms CSA, and eager customers to provide with fresh produce at the Bloomington Community Farmers' Market.

Their lives are like the lives of any farmers—lots of sun and air and backbreaking work—except that the farmers who work Heartland Farm are not like most others. They are all women, for one thing—three generations of women ranging in age from Nana (Teresa Birtles, 46) to Claira, just two years old. In between come 22-year-old Sarah McGee, mom to Claira; Jessica, who is 18; and Emily, an irrepressible eight-year-old with limitless energy, a toothy grin, and a talent for becoming best buddies with everyone she meets.

The Birtles women show up early for the Bloomington Community Farmers' Market and start unloading—cartons of eggs in palest greens, blues, pinks and browns; lovely, delicate floral bouquets assembled by Sarah; and tubs of vegetables that reflect the vibrant palette of the changing seasons, from the palest greens and lavenders in spring to the technicolor blitz of deep purples, reds, and oranges in late summer.

This bountiful display is no accident. In the winter of 1997, before deciding to market her harvest commercially, Teresa read book after book on farming and marketing. A single mom cleaning houses for a living, she was eager to raise her children in the farming life she had loved as a child, and so she stayed up late at night, evolving her own strategy for growing and selling.

She realized early on that plenty of people could outproduce her. Her farm is small, her labor force is limited, and her operations aren't mechanized, so she would have to focus on what she could do well. The Birtles women pay attention to what people want, engaging them, asking them questions, offering them choices, tempting them with samples of a bean, or an herb, or a lettuce. By listening carefully to what people say, they have been able to create a niche for themselves, producing specialty vegetables for market customers and restaurants and staying in business despite their small size and limited resources.

So Teresa reads seed catalogues and experiments, finding a bean from Italy, a gorgeous heirloom tomato, or a spicy arugula that no one else grows. You can taste her discoveries in Bloomington-area restaurants, or shop the Bloomington farmers' markets in both summer and winter to pick up some of the Heartland bounty for your own kitchen. For information on the Core Farms CSA that the Birtles participate in, see Musgrave Orchard, below.

Musgrave Orchard and Cider Mill

APPLE CIDER, RETAIL SHOP, CSA

> 8820 N. Old SR 37, Bloomington IN (Monroe)
> 812-339-5006 • www.musgraveorchard.com

There are no longer Musgraves at Musgrave Orchard, but the new owners have brought new life and new energy to the old apple trees. Andy and Amy Hamilton, who bought the orchard from Bob Musgrave in 2004 after apprenticing with him for a year, are transitioning to organic farming, a step that will make them the only commercial organic orchard in Indiana.

Most apple buyers want picture-perfect fruit, something that organic farming methods don't usually produce. But for cider the fruit's appearance isn't nearly as important as its healthfulness and taste. So the Hamiltons went cold turkey, giving up the conventional sprays that kill the bugs and prevent the diseases that plague orchards. For three years they didn't harvest an apple, but spent their time building up the soil and restoring the trees to health.

197

Currently there are 500–600 trees on their five acres—a small fraction of the huge orchard the Musgraves used to own. The Hamiltons hope to eventually get up to 1000 trees, to plant some dwarf varieties, and to find other ways to use their underutilized space. A farm market on the property gives them an outlet to sell their fresh cider (which is also available in area stores) as well as other local products, honey from their own bees, and jams, jellies, snacks, and produce.

The orchard isn't the only iron the Hamiltons have in the farming fire. On their 17-acre farm, where they live with daughters Grace and Willa, they grow vegetables to supply customers of the Core Farms CSA, an endeavor they share with fellow farmer Teresa Birtles of Heartland Family Farm (see p. 195) and occasional other partners. The CSA supplies nearly 100 families weekly during the season (May through October) with vegetables, fruit, cider, and eggs.

The combination of farming and making cider on the Orchard's antique cider press suits the Hamilton family perfectly. Amy was raised to cider making, watching her grandfather press cider, and though Andy had never picked an apple before they bought the orchard, he had a keen interest in horticulture to go along with his degree in education. Both of them had worked at Indiana University's Hilltop Garden and Nature Center, and from that experience they brought away both a commitment to farming and a desire to teach kids about gardening. They hope to someday hold a "garden camp" that will teach kids the rudiments of farming and explain to them how important it is to know where your food comes from—a lesson that Grace and Willa are already learning every day.

The market at Musgrave Orchard is open from Labor Day to Thanksgiving, Wednesdays through Sundays from 10:30 AM to 6:30 PM.

Oliver Winery

WINE

8024 North SR 37, Bloomington IN 47404 (Monroe)
812-876-5800 • www.oliverwinery.com

You could be forgiven for thinking you have strayed into

California's wine country when you first set eyes on the stunning landscaping and rustic, high-timbered tasting room of Oliver Winery, just off State Road 37, north of Bloomington. Oliver wines have come light-years from their early days in the 1960s, when Indiana University law professor William Oliver began making them in his basement. Today Oliver's son Bill and Bill's wife Kathleen head up an employee-owned operation that employs more than 75 people, harvests 37 acres of its own grapes for its Creekbend Vineyard wines, and produces more than 500,000 gallons of wine a year overall (that's something more than 210,000 cases). Oliver Winery produces nine varieties of Creekbend estate bottled wines as well as wines made from grapes grown elsewhere, hard cider, harvest fruit wines, and of course its original Camelot Mead.

It is Bill Oliver's idea that the winery should be a destination for Bloomingtonians and travelers alike—a great date place, where couples can sit out by the pond with a bottle of wine, a loaf of bread, and some great local cheese; a place where Indiana University students can bring their parents; and a place where both experienced wine aficionados and novice tasters can sip and taste and discover what Indiana's largest and oldest winery is up to these days.

What it is up to is growth and development. With a new production facility and plans for planting more acreage and maybe even building a bigger tasting room, the Olivers will be able to expand their productive capacity to as much as 250,000 cases.

Weekend visitors to Oliver can take a complimentary tour of the facilities, which includes an up-close look at a demonstration vineyard. In addition to tastings and tours, a visit to Oliver Winery can include a walk through the gorgeously landscaped grounds and a shopping spree

in the gourmet shop, which sells not just wine parapher-
nalia but also all manner of local food treats—cheeses
(Capriole Farms, Graham Farms, and Fair Oaks), sauces
(Mad Tad DeLay's Barbeque Sauces and Crazy Charlie's
Salsas), Not Just Popcorn products, Dillman Farms jams
and preserves, Mundt's fish candies, Long Elk Farm and
Double T Ranch venison sausages, Shagbark Hickory
Syrup, Laney Honey, and Walnut Grove Spring Water, as
well as items from out of state.

Oliver Winery is open Mondays through Saturdays
from 10:00 AM to 6:00 PM and Sundays from 12 noon
to 6:00 PM. Tours are offered every half hour on Fridays
and Saturdays from 12 noon to 4:30 PM and on Sundays from 1:00 to 4:30 PM. Group tours are available by
appointment.

Restaurant Tallent

RESTAURANT

208 N. Walnut St., Bloomington IN 47404 (Monroe)
812-330-9801 • www.restauranttallent.com

When Dave Tallent talks about cooking and the local ingredients he has discovered, his voice becomes almost
reverent, as though he is talking about rare jewels or exotic blooms. The venison from a Martinsville farm, the 10
pounds of fresh asparagus scored from a local farmer, the
pancetta he would cure himself, the regional cheeses—
found treasures all. His eyes light up, his cheeks turn
pinker, his voice gets hushed. The man is in love with
food.

Tallent was close to graduating from Indiana University when the lure of the kitchen sent him down a different path. Food had always been an important part of his
world, an integral part of his family life and celebrations.

He'd cooked in a wide range of Bloomington restaurants while he was in school, and he realized that cooking had become not just a way to pay the bills but something he loved. While working at the Upland Brewing Company, he met Kristen Britton, who was fated to become a pastry chef, his wife, and his partner in running Restaurant Tallent. The two got serious about cooking and headed off to study at the Culinary Institute of America (an intense, disciplined, eye-opening experience that Tallent says he'd do all over again, just for the fun of it). After that, they worked in restaurants in New York and Atlanta before coming home to open their own place.

Tallent's primary commitment in his restaurant is to providing delicious food that highlights the wonderful bounty of southern Indiana, seasonal dishes like a Caprese Terrine, made with ripe Indiana heirloom tomatoes and fresh house-made mozzarella; a Summer Melon Salad with Capriole Cheese; Pumpkin Gnocchi with Brussels Sprouts, Sage Butter, and a Cider Reduction; Fiedler Farms Pork Osso Buco with Wibs Parmesan Grits; and Elk Loin with Butternut Squash Barlotto, Caramelized Brussels Sprouts, and Bourbon Mustard Sauce (featured on p. 202).

He has an extensive network of local producers, farmers, and artisans from whom he buys as much of the food he serves as possible, and it's a rare farmers' market that doesn't see Tallent conferring with farmers, examining produce, and composing menu specials in his head as he strolls the aisles. An active member of the Slow Food movement and co-leader of Slow Food Bloomington, he puts his money where his mouth is, conducting exhaustive searches for great, organic, local foods. "That's what is in here for me," he says, putting his hand to his heart; "that's what I love."

Diners enjoy Tallent's cooking in the spare and elegant restaurant, located just off Bloomington's downtown square. An open window from the front dining room allows a peek into a surprisingly orderly and calm kitchen; those with tables nearby can watch the show while eating. A second spacious dining room opens off the first, and can be closed off for private parties. At the small bar in front, those not hungry enough for a full dinner can snack off the bar menu—a serious treat in itself.

Restaurant Tallent is open Mondays through Saturdays from 5:00 to 10:00 PM. Reservations are recommended. The bar menu is available only in the bar.

ELK LOIN WITH BUTTERNUT SQUASH BARLOTTO, CARAMELIZED BRUSSELS SPROUTS, AND BOURBON MUSTARD SAUCE

Chef Dave Tallent of Restaurant Tallent uses Long Elk Farm elk and seasonal produce in this hearty fall entrée.

Butternut Squash Barlotto
- · 2 cups pearled barley
- · 1 shallot, minced
- · 1 garlic clove, minced
- · 1 cup diced butternut squash
- · 1 tablespoon chopped fresh rosemary
- · 1 tablespoon chopped fresh sage
- · 1 tablespoon chopped parsley
- · 5 cups chicken stock
- · 2 tablespoons extra-virgin olive oil
- · 2 tablespoons butter

Brussels Sprouts
- · 24 Brussels sprouts, quartered

- 1 shallot, minced
- 1 garlic clove, minced
- 1 tablespoon chopped fresh rosemary
- 1 tablespoon chopped fresh sage
- 1 tablespoon chopped parsley
- 2 tablespoons extra-virgin olive oil
- 1 tablespoon butter
- ½ cup chicken stock

Elk Loin

- 2 pounds elk loin
- 3 tablespoons extra-virgin olive oil
- Salt and pepper to taste
- 2 tablespoons bourbon
- 2 tablespoons butter
- 1 tablespoon Dijon mustard
- 1½ cups beef broth or veal stock

For the Barlotto

Heat 1½ tablespoons olive oil and ½ teaspoon butter in a medium sauté pan. Add squash and cook 5–6 minutes, until caramelized and soft. Drain on a paper towel and add salt and pepper. Set aside.

Rinse the barley and toast it over medium heat in a dry saucepan for 6–7 minutes. Add ½ tablespoon oil and ½ tablespoon butter, shallots, and garlic and cook for 4 more minutes. Add half of the chicken stock and the salt and pepper, and stir every 2 minutes until the liquid is absorbed. Add the rest of the chicken stock and cook, continually stirring, until almost completely absorbed. Add herbs, squash, and remaining butter. Add salt and pepper to taste.

For the Sprouts

Blanch the Brussels sprouts for 2 minutes in boiling water, then remove them and shock them in a bowl of ice water. Heat a large sauté pan and add the olive oil. Drain the Brussels sprouts and cook in the oil until caramelized, about 5 minutes.

Add the shallots, garlic, chicken stock, herbs, butter, and salt and pepper. Cook over medium-high heat until the sprouts are glazed.

For the Elk

Rub the elk loin with the olive oil and sprinkle with salt and pepper. In a sauté pan, cook it 4–5 minutes on each side. This will cook it to medium rare. For medium, cook 6–7 minutes on each side. Elk meat is very lean, and Tallent does not recommend cooking it past medium, because it will become very tough.

Remove elk from the pan and take the pan off the heat. Pour in about 2 tablespoons bourbon. Place pan back on heat and flambé. Once the flame dies out, pour in 1½ cups beef broth or veal stock, scrape up any browned bits on the bottom of the pan, and simmer until reduced by half. Then whisk in 2 tablespoons of cold butter and 1 tablespoon of Dijon mustard and keep warm until other components are cooked.

To Serve

Place the barlotto in the middle of the plate and the Brussels sprouts on top. Slice the elk, lay the slices on the sprouts, and finish with the sauce. Serves 4–6.

Beiersdorfer Orchard

FRUITS, CIDER

21874 Kuebel Rd., Guilford IN 47022 (Dearborn)
812-487-2695 • www.beiersdorfer.com

Bill and Hilda Beiersdorfer, along with their children and grandchildren, work this 75-acre orchard in Dearborn County, making it a sixth-generation family farm. They grow apples, peaches, and plums and make cider year-round. Their farm market, selling orchard fruit, cider, apple butter, and other local food products like popcorn, sorghum, and honey, is open all year, Mondays through Saturdays from 9:00 AM to 6:00 PM and Sundays from 1:00 to 6:00 PM.

Bloomingfoods

MEMBER-OWNED CO-OP

East Store
3220 E. 3rd St., Bloomington IN 47401 (Monroe)
812-336-5400

Downtown Store
419 E. Kirkwood Ave., Bloomington IN 47408 (Monroe)
812-336-5300

Near West Store
316 W. 6th St., Bloomington IN 47404 (Monroe)
812-333-7312 • www.bloomingfoods.org

From the funky little downtown storefront that opened its doors on East Kirkwood in 1976 (and is still there), Bloomingfoods has thrived and expanded, adding a much larger eastside store and, in 2007, a near-westside store as well. Bloomingfoods is a member-owned cooperative grocery (one of only 400 in the nation and five in Indiana), although you needn't be a member to shop there. Bloomingfoods carries fresh (often local) organic produce, locally made or produced fruit butters and preserves, local organic eggs and dairy products, honey, maple syrup, breads, bagels, wines, beers, cheeses, and, most of the time, frozen poultry, pork, elk, lamb, goat, and buffalo—all from local farms.

205

Bloomington Brewing Company Farmstead Brewery

BEER

2687 N. Loesch Rd., Bloomington IN 47404 (Monroe)
812-339-2256 • www.bloomington.com

Jeff Mease, of the Bloomington Brewing Company, is a man with many plans. His company, One World Enterprises, already owns both the BBC and Lennie's Restaurant (1795 E. 10th St., Bloomington), as well as five Pizza Express stores. Now he's bought about 70 acres of land on the west side of Bloomington and is branching out even further, into the realms of farmstead brewing (with plans to produce a beer that that is made completely from barley and hops grown on the farm), cheese making (water buffalo mozzarella), and possibly sausage making as well. His goal is to create a destination brewery, like the wineries of southern California—a beautiful place where people can enjoy good food and beer. It's a work in progress, so call or check the website to see how his plans are coming along.

BLU Boy Chocolate Café and Cakery

BAKERY, CAFÉ

112 E. Kirkwood Ave., Bloomington IN 47404 (Monroe)
812-334-8460 • www.bluboychocolates.com

BLU Boy Chocolate Café and Cakery is a tiny jewel box of a shop filled with dazzling chocolatey gems, flakey pastries, rich chunky cookies, a tempting menu of coffee drinks, and some seriously good hot chocolate. What's more, many of these treats are made with local ingredients—a difficult feat for a bakery to pull off. The BLU Boys, owners David Fletcher and Scott Jackman, buy eggs from Heartland Family Farm, dairy products from Traders Point Creamery, and fruits, berries, and herbs for their luscious chocolates from the farmers' market.

With room for ten to sit and snack, the café is a cozy stop for morning coffee or afternoon tea. If you're lucky, the ever-changing menu may feature scones and jam and clotted cream. The Café and Cakery is open daily from 10:00 AM.

BLU BOY'S BROWN SUGAR APPLE TEA CAKE

Chef David Fletcher uses local ingredients to make this cake. You can use whatever kind of apples you like—just see what's looking good at the farmers' market.

- 1½ cups all-purpose flour
- 1 teaspoon baking powder
- Pinch of salt
- 1½ teaspoons cinnamon
- ½ teaspoon ginger
- ⅛ teaspoon cloves
- 1½ cups brown sugar
- 2 sticks butter
- 2 teaspoons vanilla
- ½ cup Traders Point Creamery Fromage Blanc
- ½ cup whole milk
- 4 large eggs
- 2 Indiana apples, peeled, cored, and diced

Preheat oven to 350°. Spray 9-inch round cake pan with nonstick cooking spray.

Combine first 6 ingredients in a mixing bowl. Whisk together eggs, fromage blanc, milk, and vanilla in another bowl. Beat butter and sugar together on medium speed until light and fluffy, approximately 5 minutes. Reduce speed to low. Beat in ⅓ of the flour mixture, then ½ of the egg/fromage blanc mixture. Scrape bowl. Repeat, and scrape bowl again. Add remainder of flour mixture and mix just until combined. Add chopped apple and stir until combined.

Scrape batter into prepared pan and bake until golden brown and a toothpick inserted into the center of the cake comes out clean, approximately 40 minutes. Cool in pan for 10 minutes, then turn onto wire rack and cool completely. Serve with whipped cream. Serves 8–10.

Brothers Beef

BEEF

1020 N. 850 E., Columbus IN 47203 (Bartholomew)
812-343-8119 • www.brothersbeef.com

Brothers Trevor and Brett Glick are the latest members of their clan to work the land that their family has owned since the 1890s. They grow corn and soy and raise a small herd of Angus beef cattle. The brothers claim that their cattle live "the way cattle are meant to live"—drug-free, pastured in summer and fed high-quality hay in winter. The beef is available in limited quantities, sold and delivered directly to the customer by the whole, half, or quarter.

The Butcher's Block

MEATS, FISH

115 South SR 46, Bloomington IN 47408 (Monroe)
812-336-6328 • www.btownbutchershop.com

What started as a project for a business school class at

Indiana University has turned into one of the Bloomington area's best sources for great meats and fish, including local choices like Fischer Farms beef (p. 162) and Cook's bison (p. 62). The Butcher's Block also sells other local artisanal products as well as house-smoked brisket, sausages, poultry, and fish. Open Mondays through Fridays from 9:00 AM to 7:00 PM and Saturdays from 8:00 AM to 6:00 PM.

Core Farms CSA

CSA

See Musgrave Orchard, p. 197, and Heartland Family Farm, p. 195.

Denny Grassfed Beef

BEEF

> 7747 Old Palmyra Rd., Pekin IN 47165 (Washington)
> 812-967-3642 • jwdenny@wcrtc.net

John Denny is the fourth generation of his family to work this farm, raising all-natural, drug-free, grass-fed beef cattle. The cattle are born and raised on the farm and fed only grass throughout their lives. The meat is processed in Memphis, Indiana, and dry-aged for tenderness and flavor. The meat is sold year-round, subject to availability, by the side, half, or quarter. You can place an order by phone and pick aged meat up at the processing plant.

Dillman Farm

FRUIT JELLIES, PRESERVES, AND BUTTERS

> 4955 West SR 45, Bloomington IN 47403 (Monroe)
> 800-359-1362 • www.dillmanfarm.com

Dillman Farms is jammin'. That's what this family-owned company does, after all, cranking out jar after gorgeous jar of jewel-toned jellies, preserves, and fruit butters. These run the gamut from the original Indiana apple butter (as well as other fruit butters like apricot, cherry, and blueberry) to jams (best-selling seedless black raspberry and strawberry, and more exotic choices like dark sweet cherry and red tomato preserves), to such sparkling clear jellies as fiery jalapeño, cinnamon cider, and red wine. All are available at area stores, online, and at Dillman Farm's onsite shop.

FarmFresh CSA

CSA

> Laughery Valley Growers, Inc.
> 407 Merkel Rd., Batesville IN 47006 (Ripley)
> 812-933-0762
> www.foodandgrowers.org/farmfreshcsa_growers

FarmFresh CSA is an initiative of the Food and Growers Association of Laughery Valley & Environs (p. 211). About ten farms join to provide subscribers in the Ripley County area with fruits, vegetables, and herbs. See the website or call for more details.

Food and Growers Association of Laughery Valley & Environs

PRODUCER GROUP

15 Red Oak Dr., Batesville IN 47006 (Ripley)
www.foodandgrowers.org

The Food and Growers Association is a farmer-owned trade cooperative that has worked since 2006 with area farmers and the community to build a market for local, sustainably produced foods. Its website catalogues and provides contact information for local producers and markets, primarily in Ripley County. The FGA helped create the FarmFresh CSA and participates in a "Buy Fresh, Buy Local" campaign.

Harvest Lodge

CATERER

441 Pine Ridge Rd., Nashville IN 47448 (Brown)
812-988-1249

The line for fresh, hot tamales at the Bloomington Community Farmers' Market is a long one, and some people even call ahead and reserve them to be sure they aren't gone before they get there. Erika Yochum makes tamales, tarts, and other baked goods from produce grown by the Harvest Lodge farm and other local farmers, and everything is delicious. Harvest Lodge caters private functions and, in addition to the summer market in Bloomington, sells at the Bloomington Winter Market and Traders Point Creamery Market.

Leane and Michael's Sugarbush

MAPLE SYRUP

321 N. Garrison Hollow Rd., Salem IN 47167 (Washington)
812-967-4491 • www.lmsugarbush.com

The hard work at Leane and Michael's Sugarbush comes in the late winter and early spring, when they tap about 2,000 trees on their Washington County farm, boil down the sap, filter the syrup, and bottle it. The fun takes place during their maple syrup festival—two weekends at the end of February and the beginning of March (see website for dates). Syrup-making demonstrations, rides in a mule-drawn wagon, activities and crafts for kids, music, and good food are the order of the day. They have syrup, maple cream, sugar cakes, and granulated sugar available in season, from January 20 to March 15, and frozen products at other times. They sell products both directly and by mail order, but call before coming by.

Local Growers Guild

PRODUCER GROUP

PO Box 2553, Bloomington IN 47402 (Monroe)
812-345-1592 • www.localgrowers.org

The Local Growers Guild is a farmers' cooperative in central and southern Indiana, founded to educate consumers and communities about the value of eating local and to support growers in their efforts to connect with and supply the community. Their *Local Growers Guide,* published annually, is an invaluable source of information on local food providers. The LGG runs the Bloomington Winter Farmers' Market in Harmony School, sponsors a "Dine Local Night," and is involved with Middleway House in the construction of a USDA-funded incubator kitchen (a professional kitchen where start-up businesses can produce food) in the old Coca-Cola factory in Bloomington.

Lost River Market and Deli

MEMBER-OWNED CO-OP

26 Library St., Paoli IN 47454 (Orange)
812-723-3093 • www.lostrivercoop.com

Founded by the Lost River Community Co-op, the Lost River Market and Deli is a brand new natural foods store in Orange County. The Co-op was founded in 2005 to bring healthy, organic, locally grown food to the community, and with the opening of the Lost River Market and Deli just two years later that intention became reality. The market offers fresh and frozen natural meats, produce, and dairy from local and regional producers, as well as other organic and natural foods. At the deli you'll find a soup and salad bar as well as ready-made sandwiches and salads.

Loveland Farms Brown County Meats

PORK, BEEF

5820 S. Shore Dr., Nashville IN 47448 (Brown)
812-988-2958

That mouthwatering aroma wafting in on the morning air at the Bloomington Farmers' Market on Saturdays, tantalizingly spicy and rich, comes from the Loveland Farms booth, where Steve Love and his family are grilling Angus burgers and pork sausages, topping them with grilled onions, peppers, and sauerkraut, and serving them to a line of hungry customers as fast as they can make them. The family runs three farms—two in Brown County and one in Lawrence—on which they raise grain-finished Black Angus cattle without drugs or hormones and all-natural hogs for the family sausage business. The Loves make nine or ten kinds of sausage—Maple Link Breakfast, Garlic Bratwurst, Sweet Wisconsin Brat, Cajun Andouille, Beer Brat, Sweet Italian, Hot Italian, Sage, Brown County Special, and Chorizo. Steve Love, the family sausage maker, is self-taught, but he says, "I really worked my tail off to learn it and I'll tell you, people rant and rave about our sausages!" The Loves do catering—cookout style, nothing fancy—and also sell their products at the Sausage Shack near Lake Lemon, on South Shore Drive. The shack is open Friday nights from 5:00 to 7:00 PM and Sundays from 12 noon to 2:00 PM, but the Loves will also come down to meet regulars who call them at other times.

Marble Hill Farm

BEEF, EGGS, PRODUCE

8101 Victor Pike, Bloomington IN 47403 (Monroe)
812-824-7877

Kip and Whitney Schlegel lead double lives—professors at Indiana University by day, and farmers during every other available hour. Their beef is hormone- and antibiotic-free (both grass- and grain-fed) and their eggs are free-range. They sell at the Bloomington Farmers' Market in both summer and winter, as well as from the farm. Call first.

Merkel Goat Farm

GOAT

> 407 Merkel Rd., Batesville IN 47006 (Ripley)
> 812-933-0762

The Merkel family has been farming for six generations. Tim and Sheila raise Boer goats for meat as well as growing vegetables and herbs. Their farm is not certified organic, but the farming is natural, safe, and pesticide-free and the animals are grass-fed. The Merkels participate in the FarmFresh CSA (see p. 210) and sell produce from their farm store and at the Batesville Farmers' Market. Goat meat is available by arrangement. The Merkels also have an onsite shop, Ye Old Farmhouse, that sells crafts, items for home and garden décor, and Indiana food products.

Nick's English Hut

RESTAURANT

> 423 E. Kirkwood Ave., Bloomington IN 47401 (Monroe)
> 812-332-4040 • www.nicksenglishhut.com

A Bloomington institution, this 80-year-old restaurant is the place to go for Chef Gregg "Rags" Rago's burgers made from Fischer Farms beef, elk burgers made with meat from Long Elk Farm, pizza, strombolis, and soups and salads made from local produce. A college town bar is an unlikely place to find a chef so committed to using local foods, but Rags says, "I have a passion for food and a passion for Nick's" that are inseparable, and a passion for supporting the local community and the local farmers as well. "I put myself on the line with the food we present here—I take it very personally," he says. "And I let the food speak for itself."

Sahara Mart

SPECIALTY GROCERY

> Downtown
> 106 E. 2nd St., Bloomington IN 47401 (Monroe)
> 812-333-0502
>
> East Store
> 2611 E. 3rd St., Bloomington IN 47403 (Monroe)
> 812-333-2737 • www.saharamart.com

With a new eastside location in addition to its original downtown home, Sahara Mart serves Bloomington with its extensive offerings of imported ingredients, organic foods, local products, and unusual and affordable beers and wines. Look for Capriole and Meadow Valley Farm cheeses, Traders Point dairy products, Fischer and Fiedler Farms meats, Rhodes Family Farm eggs, Oliver, Butler, Madison, and Huber wines, and much more. An idle hour spent wandering the aisles will yield fun and fascinating food treasures.

Salatin's Orchard

FRUITS, VEGETABLES

> 10514 Chesterville Rd., Moor's Hill IN 47032 (Dearborn)
> 812-744-3481

In 1984 Donna and Richard Salatin started planting trees in their orchard as a hobby. As Donna says with a laugh, they seem to have gotten carried away. Today they grow 24 varieties of apples (Gala, Macintosh, Mutsu, Winesap, and more), plus cherries, peaches, blueberries, pears, plums, and grapes. They also grow vegetables—everything from tomatoes and peppers in summer to Indian corn and pumpkins in the fall. The Salatins have an onsite farm market open daily from June through December, from 10:00 AM to 7:00 PM, where they sell their fruits and vegetables as well as cider, jellies, apple butter, honey, and sorghum.

Schacht Fleece Farm

LAMB, CHICKEN, TURKEY, EGGS, FLEECE

> 1470 E. Schacht Rd., Bloomington IN 47401 (Monroe)
> 812-824-6425 • www.schachtfleecefarm.com

Matt and Mandy Corry raise Icelandic sheep for fleece and meat, as well as breeding stock, on her family's farm in Monroe County. The animals are raised sustainably, without drugs or chemicals. In addition to lambs, the Corrys sell pastured chickens and eggs and Bourbon Red turkeys. Fresh chickens, individual lamb cuts, and eggs are available at the Traders Point Creamery Market, the Bloomington Saturday Morning Market, and the Bloomington Winter Market. Whole and half lambs and turkeys are available by advance order and can be picked up at the farm. The Corrys hold Open Farm Days quarterly, when customers can come to buy chicken and eggs and visit the farm. Details are posted on the website.

Seven Springs Farm

EGGS, CHICKEN, BEEF, LAMB

> 7340 W. 700 N., Carthage IN 46115 (Rush)
> 765-565-6200 • www.sevenspringsindiana.com

Seven Springs Farm, in Rush County, is the state's largest natural egg producer. Using organic, biodynamic methods on their 32 acres (although they have declined to pursue organic certification), Luella and David Porter raise drug- and chemical-free chickens in mobile chicken houses. The rich, flavor-filled eggs are sold year-round in area stores and markets and figure in the recipes of many area restaurants. Seven Springs chickens, processed on-site, are sold during the summer in area stores as well. The Porters also raise grass-fed beef and lamb, and Bourbon Red turkeys are available in the fall. Seven Springs products are also sold at Traders Point Farmers' Market.

Strangers Hill Organic Farm

VEGETABLES

> 2815 Louden Rd., Bloomington IN 47404 (Monroe)
> 812-876-6520 (home) • 812-340-1737 (cell)
> 812-322-6737 (cell) • leejones@kiva.net

At Strangers Hill Organic Farm in Bloomington, Dale and Lee Jones have been in business since 1987, and have been certified organic since 1989. They grow bedding plants, vegetables, herbs, perennials, and annuals on their 20-acre farm, selling produce Saturdays at the Bloomington Community Farmers' Market, to Bloomingfoods, and wholesale to Wild Oats/Whole Foods in Indiana, Kentucky, and Ohio. Visitors to the farm are welcome (though not on Fridays and Saturdays, when Dale and Lee are busy with the market), but call first. They warn that in bad weather their driveway can be rough for those without four-wheel drive.

Sun Circle Farm

VEGETABLES

> 3875 CR 20 W., Paoli IN 47454 (Orange)
> 812-723-2430 • anthonyblondin@yahoo.com

Anthony Blondin's business card reads, "Renewal, Re-union, and Education in Sustainable Living." His principled farming produces all kinds of gorgeous vegetables on Sun Circle Farm in Paoli, but the ones that truly stand out are the potatoes. His Yukon Golds and pink-skinned Rose Golds have buttery yellow flesh, the All Blues are deep purple throughout, the Cranberry Reds are a deep rose inside, and the Caribes are pure white inside purple skins. Together, in an herb-flecked salad glistening with oil, they are a sight to behold, defying plebian stereotypes of potato salad. Buy Anthony's produce at the Bloomington Farmers' Market on Saturday mornings. If you want to visit the farm, give him a call first.

Trulli Flatbread

RESTAURANT

> 514 E. Kirkwood Ave., Bloomington IN 47401 (Monroe)
> 812-333-2700 • www.trulliflatbread.com

Trulli Flatbread is gorgeous—light wood tables, chocolate-brown linens, and antiqued mirrors on the walls. But pride of place on the lower level is held by a huge masonry oven, custom-built of Indiana limestone for the baking of Trulli's signature flatbread. Flatbread is different from pizza, says Chef Jeff Finch, because of the quality of the ingredients (including organic flours and locally produced meats, cheeses, and vegetables), the long development of the crust (a starter ferments for two days before being added to the dough for a long rise), and the cooking method (baked in that custom-built oven, which burns kiln-dried cherry and hickory wood). Whatever the technicalities, it is delicious, as are Finch's fresh-from-the-market salads and phenomenal soups.

CAPRIOLE GOAT CHEESE TART
WITH INDIANA CORN AND
OVEN-DRIED TOMATOES

Chef Jeff Finch of Trulli Flatbread created this tart to take advantage of the best an Indiana summer has to offer—corn, tomatoes, and Capriole cheese.

Crust

· 1 cup all-purpose flour
· ½ teaspoon salt
· 4 tablespoons butter, cold
· 1½ tablespoons vegetable shortening
· 3 tablespoons ice water
· 2 tablespoons mixed fresh herbs, chopped

Custard

· 7 ounces fresh Capriole goat cheese, softened
· 6 tablespoons unsalted butter
· ½ cup sour cream
· 2 large farm eggs
· ⅔ cup fresh corn kernels (about 2 ears' worth)
· 1 cup cherry or pear tomatoes
· ½ teaspoon salt
· ¼ teaspoon pepper

Combine flour and salt. Add butter and vegetable shortening, and mix into flour by squeezing it between your fingertips until it resembles coarse cornmeal. Add ice water and herbs and continue to mix (by hand or with a food processor) until dough forms a ball. Do not overhandle it. Flatten the dough into a disk, wrap in plastic wrap, and chill for at least 30 minutes. Dough can be made ahead to this point and refrigerated overnight.

Slice tomatoes in half and place on a parchment-paper-lined baking sheet, cut side up. Roast at 200 degrees for 2 hours. Cool.

When ready to roll the dough, let it sit out for 20 minutes to soften. Preheat the oven to 375°. Roll the dough out on a floured board until it is large enough to fit into a 10-inch round tart pan with a removable bottom. Place the dough in the pan and press it up against the sides. Remove any excess. Line the crust with foil and weight it with pie weights or beans. Bake for 10 minutes. Remove the weights and foil and bake for 5 more minutes. Let crust cool completely in the pan.

Lower oven to 350°.

In a bowl, whisk together the cheese, butter, sour cream, eggs, and salt and pepper. Mix the corn kernels and dried tomatoes into the custard. Pour custard into crust and smooth top with a rubber spatula. Bake for 30 minutes until filling is set. Serve warm or at room temperature. Serves 6.

Voegeli Natural Beef

BEEF

3703 North CR 150 E., Milan IN 47031 (Ripley)
513-505-8884 • 812-654-2188
www.farmone.net

Hailing from a long line of farmers, Bob Voegeli and his wife Sharon raise beef cattle the natural way on their Ripley County farm. Starting with 12–20 calves in early spring, they use rotational grazing to keep the animals on pasture, without growth hormones or other drugs. They fill orders on the farm or deliver within 50 miles. "We're totally flexible," says Sharon. Beef is available by the whole, half, quarter, or individual cuts year-round, but customers have the greatest choice if their order is received before processing in October.

WHY SHOP AT THE FARMERS' MARKET?

Although they are a relatively new phenomenon in the United States, markets around the world have long brought farmers and consumers together. And, in fact, they are becoming remarkably trendy even here. The U.S. Department of Agriculture reports that there are more than 4,300 farmers' markets in the U.S., a 10 percent increase since 2004. It's not hard to see why.

Markets are certainly good for farmers. According to the USDA, 94 percent of all farmers nationally work their farms themselves and bring in less than $250,000 in annual receipts; 19,000 of them sell only at farmers' markets. Providing them with a place to sell their products helps to preserve an endangered way of life.

Markets are good for consumers too. We get to buy fresh, healthful food bred for taste, not shelf life. Farmers' markets give us the opportunity to buy heirloom food—vegetables, fruits, and even meats and poultry that hearken back to an older time when our food didn't have to survive long-distance travel to get to us, and when its appeal to a mass market wasn't the test of its availability. Markets remind us of what food really looks and tastes like, something we used to know in the fiber of our beings, but that we forget when all our food comes wrapped in plastic and Styrofoam.

But most of all, markets are good for that indefinable something that we call community. Shoppers and vendors at the market are in a good mood, laughing and smiling and having fun—something that you rarely see at Kroger or Marsh. Farmers get to chat with the people who are going to eat their food. They share expertise, recipes, and advice face to face. Consumers see the human side of food production and get a sense of its costs and its hazards, as well as its benefits and joys. In *Eat Here; Reclaiming Homegrown Pleasures in a Global Supermarket,* Brian Halweil reports that farmers' markets make us chatty: ten times as many conversations take place at the market than at the grocery store. Farmers' markets remind us that we are truly dependent on each other in a way that is disguised when we only buy our food at the grocery store.

Of course, not all farmers' markets are created equal. Many are producer-only markets; they require, with varying degrees of strictness, that the vendor who sells the food be the one who grew or raised it. Producer-only markets create that community between grower and consumer that can be so important. But producer-only markets can be limiting—for instance, they rarely allow processed food to be sold unless the vendor produced all of its components, which usually eliminates jams and jellies (unless the vendor has a handy sugar plantation tucked away somewhere) and baked goods.

Proponents of producer-only markets like the Bloomington Community Farmers' Market (p. 188), the largest producer-only market in the state, argue that the restriction is important because otherwise vendors who are merely wholesale buyers can sell at the market. The link between farmer and consumer disappears and the market is on a slippery slope that can end up with something that looks remarkably like a grocery store.

On the other hand, markets that don't have a producer-only rule can offer a wider range of goods and can obtain fresh produce year-round. The newly built American Countryside Market (p. 46), the largest farmers' market in the Midwest, emphasizes local producers and local products, but farmers may hire someone to sell their goods and, as the website makes a point of saying, the market will have fresh produce all year round, even when vendors must import it from the southern hemisphere. Consumers get fresh local produce much of the year, and the market remains a viable concern during the colder months.

Hoosiers are lucky that they have a range of farmers' markets to choose from. There are nearly 100 in the state, and their number is growing all the time. As always, when you want to know where your food came from and how it was raised, ask questions! More than anything else, shopping at farmers' markets ensures that you are buying from people who know the answers.

EATING LOCAL WHILE DINING OUT

BLU Boy Chocolate Café and Cakery
112 E. Kirkwood Ave., Bloomington IN 47404 (Monroe)
812-334-8460 • www.bluboychocolates.com
See p. 206

FARMbloomington
108 E. Kirkwood Ave., Bloomington IN 47408 (Monroe)
812-323-0002 • www.farm-bloomington.com
See p. 192

Lennie's
1795 E. 10th St., Bloomington IN 47408 (Monroe)
812-323-2112 • www.bbc.bloomington.com

Limestone Grille
2920 E. Covenanter Dr., Bloomington IN 47401 (Monroe)
812-335-8110 • www.limestonegrille.com

MCL West Bloomington
Liberty Crossing
2100 Liberty Dr., Bloomington IN 47403 (Monroe)
812-336-2119 • www.mclhomemade.com

Nick's English Hut
423 E. Kirkwood Ave., Bloomington IN 47408 (Monroe)
812-332-4040 • www.nicksenglishhut.com
See p. 215

Restaurant Tallent
208 N. Walnut Ave., Bloomington IN 47404 (Monroe)
812-330-9801 • www.restauranttallent.com
See p. 200

Roots Vegetarian Restaurant and Juice Bar
126½ N. Walnut St., Bloomington IN 47404 (Monroe)
812-336-7668

The Story Inn
6404 South SR 135, Nashville IN 47448 (Brown)
800-881-1183 • www.storyinn.com

The Superburger
600 W. Main St., Paoli IN 47454 (Orange)
812-723-4445

Trulli Flatbread
514 E. Kirkwood Ave., Bloomington IN 47408 (Monroe)
812-333-2700 • www.trulliflatbread.com
See p. 219

Tutto Bene Wine Café & More
213 S. Rogers St., Bloomington IN 47404 (Monroe)
812-330-1060 • www.bloomingtonwinecafe.com

FARMERS' MARKETS

Batesville Farmers' Market
Intersection of Main and George Streets
Batesville IN 47006 (Ripley)
May–October, Saturdays 8:00 AM to 12 noon

Bloomingfoods Farmers' Market
3220 E. 3rd St., Bloomington IN 47401 (Monroe)
May–October, Wednesdays and Saturdays 7:00 AM to 12 noon

Bloomington Community Farmers' Market
401 N. Morton St., Bloomington IN 47404 (Monroe)
April–November, Saturdays (April–September) 8:00 AM
    to 1:00 PM, Saturdays (October–November) 9:00 AM to
    1:00 PM, Tuesdays (June–September) 3:00 to 6:00 PM
bloomington.in.gov (See p. 188)

Bloomington Winter Farmers' Market
Harmony School
909 E. 2nd St., Bloomington IN 47401 (Monroe)
January–March, Saturdays 9:00 AM to 12 noon

Columbus Farmers' Market (The Commons)
332 Commons Mall, Columbus IN 47201 (Bartholomew)
May–October, Saturdays 8:00 AM to 1:00 PM

Columbus Farmers' Market (Jackson Street)
Jackson Street between 2nd and 3rd Streets
Columbus IN 47201 (Bartholomew)
June–August, Thursdays 2:30 to 5:30 PM

Community Harvest Marketplace
201 E. 2nd St., Carthage IN 46115 (Rush)
May–October, Fridays and Saturdays 7:00 AM to
    4:00 PM, Sundays 11:00 AM to 4:00 PM

Downtown Seymour Farmers' Market
Corner of Walnut St. and St. Louis Ave.
Seymour IN 47274 (Jackson)
April–October, Wednesdays and Saturdays 7:00 AM to 12 noon

Greensburg Farmers' Market
150 Courthouse Square, Greensburg IN 47240 (Decatur)
May–October, Fridays 2:00 to 6:00 PM
www.downtowngreensburg.com

Jennings County Farmers' Market
North Vernon City Park
604 N. State St., North Vernon IN 47265 (Jennings)
May–October, Mondays 2:00 to 5:00 PM, Wednesdays
    and Saturdays 8:00 AM to 1:00 PM

Orange County Home Grown Farmers' Market
West side of Congress Square Park
Orleans IN 47452 (Orange)
May 25–October 27, Saturdays 8:00 AM to 12 noon
www.orangecountyhomegrown.org

Home Grown Indiana

Ripley County Farmers' Market (Milan)
Milan Community Park Shelter
Milan IN 47031 (Ripley)
July–September, Wednesdays 4:00 to 7:00 PM

Ripley County Farmers' Market (Osgood)
524 W. Beech St., Osgood IN 47037 (Ripley)
June–October, Saturdays 8:00 AM to 12 noon

Valley Farmers' Market
Maple Street parking lot (downtown)
French Lick IN 47432 (Orange)
May–October, Thursdays 1:00 to 6:00 PM
www.orangecountyhomegrown.org

WINERIES

Brown County Winery
4520 SR 46 E., Nashville IN 47448 (Brown)
812-988-6144 • www.browncountywinery.com

Butler Winery and Vineyard
6200 E. Robinson Rd., Bloomington IN 47408 (Monroe)
812-332-6660 • www.butlerwinery.com

Carousel Winery
8987 SR 37 S., Bedford IN 47421 (Lawrence)
812-277-9750 • www.carouselwinery.com

Chateau Pomije
25060 Jacob Rd., Guilford IN 47022 (Dearborn)
812-623-3332 • www.chateaupomijewinery.com

Ertel Cellars Winery
3794 East CR 1100 N., Batesville IN 47006 (Ripley)
812-933-1500 • www.ertelcellarswinery.com

French Lick Winery
8331 West SR 56, Suite 2, West Baden Springs IN 47469 (Orange)
812-936-2293 • www.frenchlickwinery.com

Oliver Winery
8024 North SR 37, Bloomington IN 47404 (Monroe)
812-876-5800 • www.oliverwinery.com
See p. 198

Simmons Winery
8111 E. 450 N., Columbus IN 47203 (Bartholomew)
812-546-0091 • www.simmonswinery.com

Vinetree Farm Winery
8343 W. Hardinsburg Rd., Hardinsburg IN 47125 (Washington)
812-472-3580 • www.vinetreefarm.net

MICROBREWS & BREWPUBS

Bloomington Brewing Company
1795 E. 10th St., Bloomington IN 47408 (Monroe)
812-323-2112 • www.bbc.bloomington.com
See p. 206

Power House Brewing Company
322 4th St., Columbus IN 47201 (Bartholomew)
812-375-8800 • www.powerhousebrewingco.com

Upland Brewing Company
350 W. 11th St., Bloomington IN 47404 (Monroe)
812-336-2337 • www.uplandbeer.com

FOOD FESTIVALS

Applefest
Celebration of the apple harvest, food, activities, crafts, games
Batesville IN (Ripley)
End of September
812-934-3201

Berry Fest (formerly Raspberry Fest)
Berries, berries, berries
Batesville IN (Ripley)
Early June
812-934-3101 • www.batesvillein.com

Jackson County Watermelon Festival
Watermelon games, contests, and eating
Burlington IN (Jackson)
Mid-September
812-358-2930

Leane and Michael's Sugarbush Annual Maple Syrup Festival
Tours of syrup making and maple-related eating
Salem IN (Washington)
Late February/Early March
877-841-8851 • www.lmsugarbush.com
See p. 212

Mitchell Persimmon Festival
Persimmon pudding and other foods
Mitchell IN (Lawrence)
End of September
812-849-4441 • www.mitchell-indiana.org

National Maple Syrup Festival
Tours, demonstrations, and maple treats
Medora IN (Jackson)
1st of March
812-966-2168 • www.nationalmaplesyrupfestival.com

The Week of Chocolate
Chocolate and wine tasting, contests, samples
Bloomington IN (Monroe)
End of January/Beginning of February
812-332-9615 • www.weekofchocolate.com

Week of Chocolate
Activities, eating, and exhibiting—all inspired by chocolate
Nashville (Brown)
Late January/Early February
800-753-3255 • www.weekofchocolate.com

7

Ohio

Jefferson   Switzerland

Clark

Crawford   Floyd

SOUTHERN

Vander-   Warrick   Spencer   Perry   Harrison
burgh

Posey

Southern:
The River Counties

The Ohio River provides a neat, if winding, boundary between the southern part of Indiana on one side and northern
Kentucky and a tiny bit of southwestern Ohio on the other.
Sometimes that boundary is nearly impenetrable—communities that would otherwise have easy traffic with another
state are instead tucked against the high banks of the river,
and their inhabitants are isolated, unable, unless they are
near a bridge, to go anywhere easily except north, deeper into
the Hoosier state.

Where a community is near a network of bridges, of
course, residents can cross easily. Parts of Clark and Floyd
Counties are suburbs of Louisville—and the farmers in those
counties are as likely to provide ingredients to Kentucky restaurants as to Indiana ones. They frequently sell at Louisville
markets as well as their own. In these counties, you'd think
the food traditions from Kentucky and Indiana would begin
to merge.

Not necessarily. While Kentucky has a rich history as a
distiller of whiskey, the only whiskey distillery in Indiana was
in Lawrenceburg (in Dearborn County, outside of Cincin-
nati), and it belonged to Seagram, not exactly a locally owned
producer. In any case, in 2000 Seagram's alcoholic beverage
business was bought by Pernod Ricard, which sold the Law-
renceville distillery to the CL Financial Group, which owns
Angostura, in 2007. Still not so local. There is a distillery
in Starlight (Clark County, see p. 241), but it makes fruit
brandy, not whiskey. We couldn't even track down a good
backyard still.

Kentucky has a rich tradition of smoking hams and bacon, too, but few businesses in Indiana do the same (though the two we found—one in Evansville [p. 246] and one in Jeffersonville [p. 250]—are definitely worth a visit). And Kentucky barbeque is wonderful, but again, the river seems to be an impassable barrier when it comes to some foodways.

But southern Indiana has food traditions of its own. In certain pockets they still love their snapper (turtle) soup, though that's not really a restaurant item and it can be darn hard to find. Brain sandwiches, too, are a Hoosier delicacy, especially around the Evansville area. Served battered and fried, on a hamburger bun, this treat can be found at the Hilltop Inn (1100 Harmony Way, Evansville, 812-422-1757) and at the West Side Nut Club Fall Festival (also in Evansville; www.nutclub.org). And then there is the fish candy, perhaps named for the fish that swim the river (or perhaps not). It is alive and well at Mundt's in Madison (p. 247) and Schimpff's in Jeffersonville (p. 249).

So southern Indiana does have its quirky food loves, but not many involving locally produced foods. There are some terrific producers in the area, though, and perhaps that will change. In the meantime, enjoy a drive along the river and track down some of these great finds.

Bettinger Potato Chips and Tell City Pretzel Company

KETTLE CHIPS AND HAND-TWISTED PRETZELS

248 13th St., Tell City IN 47586 (Perry)
812-547-5665 • www.bettingerchips.com
812-547-4631 • www.tellcitypretzels.com

Down in Tell City, James and Joann Simpson have acquired two venerable companies that take pains to make munchies the old-fashioned way. Crafted by hand, from first-class, partly local ingredients, the kettle chips and hand-twisted pretzels they turn out may be great for snacking, but it's a little hard to think of them as junk food.

When you step into the building that today houses the Bettinger Potato Chip Company (founded in 1917) and the Tell City Pretzel Company (1858), you find yourself right in the thick of the potato-chip side of the operation. Before your eyes, locally grown potatoes are stripped of their skins in a machine that essentially sands off the peel. They are sliced up, plunged into a kettle of boiling oil, and fried to a delicate crisp. When they are done they are turned out onto a counter, salted, and hand-sorted to ensure that only the choicest chips make it into the bag. Even the rejects look and smell tempting, and you know you could never eat just one. Bettinger Chips come in plain, barbeque, and sour cream and onion flavors.

In the huge room next door, old-fashioned pretzels are hand-twisted with equally scrupulous care and run through hot ovens to produce crunchy, crackly pretzels. Their recipe has been a closely guarded secret since the company's founding by Swiss baker Casper Gloor. An earlier owner of the factory bought a fancy pretzel-twisting machine to make the job easier, but the pretzels

Southern Indiana: The River Counties

233

didn't seem to taste the same, so the company went back to hand-twisting and the pretzel fans were content. Tell City pretzels are brittle, hard, salty, and addictive. True salt fiends like the extra-salty versions, and spice addicts can try the hot and spicy version or the very garlicky garlic pretzels. And all is not savory in pretzel land—in the cooler months there are milk- and white-chocolate-covered pretzels too.

Visit the factory to watch the process, or to pick up some fresh and crispy snacks. Owner James Simpson welcomes company and will be delighted to show you around. The factory is open Mondays through Fridays from 8:00 AM to 5:00 PM and Saturdays from 8:00 AM to 12 noon. Chips and pretzels are also available by mail order and at some area groceries and restaurants.

Blue River Café

RESTAURANT

128 Main St., Milltown IN 47145 (Crawford)
812-633-7510 • www.bluerivercafe.com

You have to be looking for the Blue River Café—the chances that you will otherwise stumble on this charming place with a fabulous restaurant, tucked away in Milltown, are slim. The café is located in a two-story white house on Main Street in Milltown, just past a pizza place and a canoe landing (where there are plenty of canoes for rent). The downstairs houses a tiny, rustic bar and an airy, blue-trimmed dining room; upstairs there are more tables and a stage for live music. Music is a big deal at the Blue River Café, but truthfully, food is the biggest deal of all.

Chef Debbie Woods and her husband, bartender and English teacher Mark, own the place and have run it for

17 years. Debbie got her training in Louisville at Sullivan College, but food is more than an academic subject to her. "Many people never realize what an emotional, spiritual, and healing thing food can be. It is what makes it all worth it to me," she says.

Debbie's cooking is bright and vibrant with seasonal flavors, and local produce is key to making it taste right. She says, "We use local produce and eggs whenever we can get them. We have some very good farmers in our area and we live in a very fertile place. We change the menu every weekend in order to accommodate whatever is available locally. Mostly, we just know that what we grow locally always tastes best!" Produce comes from their own garden (they used to sell produce to Louisville restaurants, but now they keep it all for their own), from Churchill's Countryside Market down State Road 64 (see p. 245), and from other local farms.

The Blue River Café has a permanent menu of standbys—lots of sandwiches, including burgers and vegetarian options, and salads. The burger platter comes with excellent celery-seed-laden coleslaw and hand-cut steak fries. Note that these are not the dry and flakey kind of fries with too much potato, not enough fry. They have a twice-cooked creaminess to them and are sliced thin and fried crispy, so there is plenty of crunch as well as potato. There is also a weekly lunch and dinner menu that changes with what's in season. The weekly menu is available online—it might include some great soups, prime rib, and ribeye steak, as well as several fish and vegetarian selections, plus seasonal side dishes.

The beer and wine list is also really good, and the music filtering down the stairs into the main dining room is always pleasant. It takes a smidge over an hour to get to the Blue River Café from Bloomington, and it's a relaxing drive through the country—no interstate, no diesel, just lots of farms and horses and cows and cornfields for a lovely, soothing Indiana road trip.

The Blue River Café is open Thursdays through Saturdays for lunch and dinner from 11:00 AM to 10:00 PM and on Sundays for brunch and early dinner from 11:00 AM to 8:00 PM. Check out the website for menu and entertainment details.

SAUTÉED SUMMER SQUASH WITH TOMATO BASIL VINAIGRETTE

Chef Debbie Woods of the Blue River Café gets all the flavors of summer on the plate with this vibrant side dish.

- *2 cups chopped ripe tomatoes*
- *1 clove garlic, minced*
- *1 tablespoon onion, finely diced*
- *¼ cup fresh basil, chopped*
- *3 tablespoons raspberry vinegar*
- *Pinch sugar*
- *Salt and pepper to taste*
- *½ cup olive oil*
- *2 tablespoons butter*
- *2 medium yellow squash, sliced or julienned*
- *2 medium zucchini, sliced or julienned*

Whisk the first eight ingredients together. Set aside.

In a medium-heavy skillet or pan, melt butter. Sauté squash over medium-high heat until softened and edges are browned and begin to caramelize.

Pour vinaigrette over sautéed squash. Serve warm or at room temperature. Serves 4.

Capriole Farm

GOAT CHEESE

10329 Newcut Rd., Greenville IN 47124 (Floyd)
812-923-9408 • www.capriolegoatcheese.com

A capriole is a playful kick, a frolic in the air, a twist, a turn, a caper. Baby goats are prone to such antics—in fact, the Latin word *caper* (from which comes "capriole") means "goat." When Judy Schad was looking for a name for her goat farm in the southern Indiana hills, she chose Capriole, she says, because a capriole is "a happy, happy thing."

That's fitting, because making goat cheese is, by and large, a happy, happy business for Schad. It is hard work too, of course; despite the cartoon image of the hearty goat out in the field chewing on old boots and spitting out nails, goats are the most fragile of the milk animals. But still, Schad loves them all, cuddling the newborns, spoiling favorite does in their declining years, enjoying a ribald chuckle over the ripe and randy bucks, and nurturing all 300 of her animals into producing plenty of milk for her cheeses.

Shoppers at the Bloomington Farmers' Market know Judy Schad well. She's the one wearing lipstick and pearls on Saturday mornings, with dark, laughing eyes and a fast, chatty drawl, spearing up samples of goat cheese for customers to taste, perhaps with a bit of ripe juicy peach or rich red tomato, and talking all the while—maybe holding three conversations at once, maybe losing track of one or two of them, but somehow ending up at the right place: with a smile and a sale and a satisfied customer.

Satisfied with good reason. Goat cheese (known also by its French name, *chèvre*) is distinctive, its unmistakable tang a piquant reminder that this cheese did not come from a cow or a sheep. And Capriole goat cheese is among the very best, from the fresh, soft cheeses that spread on crusty bread like cream cheese, to the heady aged cheeses, covered with ash or soft downy mold or herbs and spices or a bourbon-soaked chestnut leaf, to the more assertive washed-rind cheeses that combine a hint of the barnyard with the kick of the goat.

For those who know cheese, Schad's are the cream; they have won multiple American Cheese Society awards and cheese guru Steve Jenkins, author of *The Cheese Primer,* calls them "national treasures." They've been written up everywhere from *The New Yorker* to *People* magazine, and they appear on the menus of top restaurants across the country—from Campanile and Providence in Los Angeles, to the Everest Room and Charlie Trotter's in Chicago, to Picholine and Le Cirque and Le Bernadin in New York.

But if Schad's cheeses are national treasures, they are also Indiana's own. Schad and her lawyer husband Larry both grew up in New Albany, and they raised their three children on the farm in Greenville where she has been making goat cheese since 1982.

Capriole cheese is available at many area grocery stores, at the Bloomington Saturday summer and winter farmers' markets, at Broad Ripple Market, by mail order, and at the onsite farm store, open Mondays through Fridays from 9:00 AM to 3:00 PM. Call first to be sure someone is there.

HERBED MARINATED GOAT CHEESE

This recipe from Judy Schad's kitchen makes a savory appetizer. Vary quantities of cheese and herbs to suit your taste and serve with plenty of crusty bread to soak up the flavorful oil.

- 1 pound Chantal Apéritifs or other small fresh goat cheeses
- Several roasted garlic cloves
- ½ teaspoon dried basil
- ½ teaspoon dried thyme
- ½ teaspoon dried rosemary
- good olive oil, or olive oil/canola oil mix

Place cheese in a sterile jar with garlic, basil, thyme, and rosemary. Cover with oil, put top on jar, and refrigerate. Allow to marinate for at least a week for cheese to absorb oil and flavor from herbs and garlic.

Refrigerated, the cheese will keep for several months. Allow to come to room temperature before use and serve as an appetizer or light lunch with crusty baguette and olives on the side, or on a salad.

When cheese is gone, the remaining oil can be mixed with a good balsamic vinegar for a wonderful salad dressing.

Fiedler Family Farms

BEEF, LAMB, PORK

14056 East SR 66, Rome IN 47574 (Perry)
812-836-4348 • www.fiedlerfamilyfarms.com

Rebekah Fiedler was getting impatient with the hear-no-evil, see-no-evil attitude of a customer at the Bloomington Farmers' Market who didn't want to know how she raised her lambs. "Come on, Rebekah, can't you just pretend that you found this roast out in the field, all freezer-wrapped and ready to sell?" pleaded the market-goer, trying to block out images of cute and fleecy lambs.

"Look," said Fiedler, in the tone one uses to speak to very young, very obstinate children, "my animals have a wonderful life. They live in the open air, they eat what nature designed them to eat, and they can run and play to their hearts' content. Their life is good. They just have one really bad day."

Clearly Fiedler and her husband Jim are proud of the way they raise their animals, and they have cause. When you visit their beautiful farm, it's clear that the animals do indeed lead wonderful lives. The squealing piglets and their massive mothers, grunting maternal directions at them, look as happy as only pigs splashing around in mud can look. The huge cattle, ushered from one field to another in the Fiedlers' rotational grazing system, chew grass with a kind of bovine contentment that makes sense.

In fact, the Fiedlers use holistic and humane methods to raise their Angus, Red Devon, and Hereford beef cattle, their Katahdin sheep, and their Large Black pigs. No drugs or chemicals are used on the animals; there are no herbicides or pesticides in the fields. The cattle are fed grass their entire lives, and the pigs are pastured, resulting in rich, marbled, flavorful meat.

Although they are the third generation of Fiedlers to farm this land, Jim and Rebekah came back to farming from big-city careers in New York. Rebekah was home on maternity leave from her job in the World Trade Center on September 11, 2001, and the horror of what might have been convinced them to come home and live a different life.

Today the stresses of making a living from the farm are real, but the life is rewarding. The Fiedlers are passionate about the benefits of raising their animals on pasture (Rebekah is the Swine Director of the American Grassfed Association) and committed to giving the animals a good and healthy life on the farm. (See "Why Grass-Fed Beef?" on p. 251.) And if the animals have only one really bad day, well, how many of us are lucky enough to make that claim, after all?

The Fiedlers sell their meats at the Bloomington Community Farmers' Market, at the Bloomington Winter Farmers' Market, at the Tell City Market (Wednesdays from 3:00 to 6:00 PM), at Beargrass Farmers' Market in Louisville (Tuesdays from 3:00 to 7:00 PM), occasionally at Bardstown Road Farmers' Market in Louisville (Saturdays from 8:00 AM to 12 noon), and from their farm. Call ahead to be sure someone is there.

Huber's Orchard, Winery, and Vineyards

FRUIT, VEGETABLES, WINE

> 19816 Huber Rd., Starlight IN 47106 (Clark)
> 812-923-9463 • www.huberwinery.com
> www.starlightdistillery.com

The story of the successful family farm is often a story of diversification—finding a way to take a seasonal business that is subject to the whims of Mother Nature and market forces and put your eggs, so to speak, in enough baskets that you aren't overset if disaster strikes some of them. The Huber family has done that with a vengeance—taking the family farm from orchard, to dairy farm, to fruits and vegetables, to Christmas trees, to winery, to distillery. Seven generations of Hubers have found a home on the family's acreage—now expanded to almost 600 from the original 80 that were planted in 1843 by Simon Huber, newly arrived from Germany with seven apple trees.

Today, Huber's is a farm market, selling all kinds of berries, peaches, tomatoes, corn, summer squash, and, in the fall, apples and pumpkins galore (and Christmas trees, in season); a bakery; a Children's Farm Park; an ice cream factory; a cheese shop (though cheese is no longer made onsite); a winery, offering tastings and wine tours; a winery café, offering sandwiches and snacks of cheese and sausage; and a distillery, producing artisanal brandies.

The something-for-everyone approach makes this a good family destination; the Fun Park has all kinds of activities for kids, while adults can keep busy sampling the fruits of the largest estate bottled winery in Indiana and the first native Indiana distillery.

The vineyard produces more than 400,000 pounds of 18 varieties of grapes a year and turns them into award-winning wines (a full list is available online). Daily complimentary wine tours take you from the harvest and processing of the grapes to the aging rooms and then to the bottling lines. More in-depth and specialized tours can be arranged for a fee.

The newest addition to the Huber enterprises is the distillery. After years of planning, learning the craft, and getting legislation passed that would allow this Hoosier winery to produce brandy as well, the Hubers released their first bottles in 2004. They make grappa and fruit brandies, and they have experimented with infusing their brandies and wines together, producing Blueberry Port, Raspberry Infusion, Peach Nectar, Apple Infusion, and Pear Infusion.

The winery, ice cream shop, and farm market are open year-round, Mondays through Saturdays from 10:00 AM to 6:00 PM and Sundays from 12 noon to 6:00 PM. Call to check on extended hours and holiday closings. The Children's Farm Park is open May 1 through November 30 from 10:00 AM to 5:00 PM. Call or email to arrange a distillery tour.

Joe Huber Family Farm and Restaurant

RESTAURANT, MARKET, U-PICK

2421 Scottsville Rd., Starlight IN 47106 (Clark)
812-923-5255 • 877-JOE-HUBERS (563-4823)
www.joehubers.com

Hubers are thick on the ground in Starlight. Not far from the Huber Orchard and Winery is the Joe Huber Family Farm and Restaurant—a U-Pick farm, market, and family-style eatery where enormous and delicious helpings of fried chicken, country ham, and garden-fresh veggies take you back to a time untouched by the fast-food world of today.

Patriarch Joe Huber (Joe Jr., that is) died in early 2008. His wife, Bonnie, their five kids, and *their* kids, the seventh generation of Hubers, all live and work on the farm that Joe Sr. bought in 1926. You don't need to read Joe's book, *Winning with Family,* to know that family matters to these folks. A lot.

Joe was working his small, conventional family farm, struggling to earn a living by selling to area wholesalers, when, in the 1960s, he got the idea to cut out the middlemen and sell directly to the public as a U-Pick operation. He could charge more than wholesalers would pay, and customers would get to enjoy a day in the country and still get a better price than they'd get in the stores. Skeptics warned him that it wouldn't work, but by the early '70s crowds of people were arriving, eager to pick their own green beans and strawberries, and the Hubers had found a way to save the farm.

That same ingenuity came in handy when, in the '80s, it was apparent that, with more women in the workforce, families were eating out more often and had less time to cook and preserve foods at home. Bonnie had begun serving home-cooked meals to farm visitors, and those meals proved so popular that in 1983 the Hubers broke ground on their own restaurant.

Today that restaurant thrives. Whole families arrive to pick their own berries, apples, and pumpkins (or to buy them ready-picked in the market) and to explore the farm and the flower gardens. There are ducks to feed and animals to pet, and when everyone is hungry they can settle in for a hearty meal. The restaurant offers a full menu of appetizers (be sure to try the fried green tomatoes), sandwich platters, and country-style suppers, but the house specialty is the Country Platter Dinner: plates of fried chicken, Huber Honey Ham, fried biscuits with apple butter, mashed potatoes and gravy, green beans and corn, and chicken and dumplings, all served family-style. You'll be way too full for homemade pie, but don't let that stop you.

The restaurant is open year-round (except between December 24 and January 1), Mondays through Saturdays from 11:00 AM to 8:00 PM, Sundays and holidays from 11:00 AM to 6:00 PM. The farm market and gift shop are open January–April, Saturdays and Sundays from 12 noon to 5:00 PM; May to October, Mondays through Saturdays from 8:00 AM to 8:00 PM, Sundays and holidays from 10:00 AM to 6:00 PM; November 1 through December 23, Sundays through Thursdays (and holidays) from 10:00 AM to 6:00 PM, Fridays and Saturdays from 10:00 AM to 8:00 PM.

Bryant's Blueberries

BLUEBERRIES

6900 Oak Park Rd. N.E., New Salisbury IN 47161 (Harrison)
812-366-3592 • www.bryantsblueberries.com

Dale and Diane Bryant's blueberry farm is a family-owned U-Pick operation about half an hour from Louisville. The crop is minimally sprayed, but not certified organic. You can sign up for email updates on the availability of the harvest on their website, where the Bryants have also collected some choice blueberry recipes.

Bud's Farm Market

VEGETABLES

> 3301 S. Weinbach Ave., Evansville IN 47714 (Vanderburgh)
> 812-477-3070 • www.budsfarm.com

Bud Vogt's farm has been in the family for more than 50 years, and the third generation is in the process of taking over. While the farm is not certified organic, the Vogts grow their vegetables naturally. The main crop is tomatoes—more than 20 varieties, from hothouse to heirloom—but they do grow other vegetables as well, and they are known for experimenting with unusual varieties. They sell to two local all-natural grocery stores and also have a market on the farm, where they sell their own and other locally grown produce. The market is open Mondays through Saturdays from 8:30 AM to 6:00 PM and Sundays from 10:00 AM to 5:00 PM.

Churchill's Countryside Market

FRUITS, VEGETABLES

> 4075 SR 64 N.W., DePauw IN 47115 (Harrison)
> 812-347-3486

Three generations of Churchills have worked this family farm, producing sweet corn, peppers, squash, zucchini, cucumbers, melons, tomatoes, and other fruits and vegetables. The produce is sold from 9:00 AM to 6:00 PM daily at the onsite farm market, right on State Road 64, from July 10 through October 31. The farm also supplies area restaurants like the Blue River Café, up the road in Milltown (see p. 234). The farm also offers U-Pick, wagon rides to the pumpkin patch, and a festival on the second Sunday in October. Call for details.

Holiday World and Splashin' Safari

RESTAURANTS

> 452 E. Christmas Blvd., Santa Claus IN 47579 (Spencer)
> 877-463-2645 • www.holidayworld.com

Most locavores would not expect to find much local flavor at a theme park, especially one with more than 1,000,000 visitors a year, feeding most of them several times a day. That's why it comes as such a pleasant surprise to learn that Holiday World and Splashin' Safari use local foods as often as possible. When produce is in season, if it's grown in Indiana you'll probably find it on the menu at their 17 different eateries. At the ZOOMbabwe Grill, you will even find a moist and delicious Dewig Meats (see p. 174) pork chop sandwich. A full listing of the parks' eateries, with menus, is available on the website.

Mayse Farm Market

VEGETABLES, SMOKED HAMS, SAUSAGES

> 6400 N. Saint Joseph Ave., Evansville IN 47720 (Vanderburgh)
> 812-963-3175 • www.maysefarmmarket.com

Paul and Sherrill Mayse farm the land that's been in the family since 1951. Their produce season begins with May's strawberries and the tomatoes that come from their four greenhouses, and goes on through October's pumpkins. In the fall they start up the other part of the business, buying sides of local hogs from Jasper and processing the meat themselves. The Mayses cure and smoke their own hams and bacon and make liver sausage, fresh and smoked sausages, and pon haus (scrapple). The onsite bakery turns out fruit breads (zucchini, apple, banana, and strawberry, in season), six varieties of pies, and cobblestone bread. The market is open nine months of the year, May 1 to January 31, Mondays through Saturdays from 8:30 AM to 6:00 PM and Sundays from 10:00 AM to 4:00 PM. Check the website to see what is available.

Mundt's

CANDY

207 W. Main St., Madison IN 47250 (Jefferson)
812-265-6171 • www.mundtscandies.com

The first Mundt's Candy Store in Madison opened in 1893 and, except for a break from 1966 to 1998, one has been open ever since. Today the business is an old-fashioned ice cream parlor and a candy manufacturer specializing in that peculiar southern Indiana specialty, fish candy. In the shape of fish and in a variety of flavors, these candies have been made and eaten in Ohio river towns since the mid-1880s. Mundt's candy is sold in the shop (seasonal hours, call for information) and by mail order. Of course, you need to be there in person to get "The '37 Flood," a formidable ice cream sundae that serves four to six people, topped with—what else?—a chocolate fish.

Ohio River Valley Food Venture

SHARED-USE COMMERCIAL KITCHEN

975 Industrial Dr., Madison IN 47250 (Jefferson)
812-265-3135

The Ohio River Valley Food Venture's kitchen gives local entrepreneurs the opportunity to process food in an inspected and certified facility. The staff helps ensure that the food made in it meets FDA requirements, and they also help with marketing. Foods made in the kitchen include baked goods, salad dressings, sauces, salsas, jams, and jellies—anything but meat. The Ohio River Valley Food Venture encourages the use of local ingredients. While clients are responsible for bringing in their own food, the kitchen can order it and have it shipped directly, often from local producers.

Richmer Farms

FRUIT, VEGETABLES

3561 Lazy Creek Rd., Lanesville IN (Harrison)
812-952-8844

Donald Richmer runs this fifth-generation farm. It is a Hoosier Homestead, which means that the Indiana State Department of Agriculture certifies that the farm has been in the same family for at least 100 years. He has set up a small retail market to sell strawberries, pumpkins, and mums in season. The market is open from 10:00 AM until 7:00 PM.

River City Food Co-op

MEMBER-OWNED CO-OP

116 Washington Ave., Evansville IN 47713 (Vanderburgh)
812-401-7301 • www.www.rivercityfoodcoop.org

Founded in 2005, the River City Co-op has grown rapidly and provides a downtown alternative to conventional grocery shopping. Open to the public, it sells natural, organic, and bulk grocery items. It is committed to buying local whenever possible, so it offers local cheeses, meats, eggs, and seasonal vegetables. The co-op is open Mondays through Thursdays from 10:00 AM to 7:00 PM, Saturdays from 9:00 AM to 5:00 PM, and Sundays from 12 noon to 5:00 PM.

Schimpff's Confectionery

CANDY

347 Spring St., Jeffersonville IN 47130 (Clark)
812-283-8367 • www.schimpffs.com

Schimpffs have been making candy at this mom-and-pop candy store with the old-fashioned soda fountain since 1891 (and across the river in Louisville even before that). Local favorites like cinnamon redhots, hard candy fish (p. 247), and Modjeskas (caramel-covered marshmallows— a tradition along the Ohio River) are joined by chocolate, caramel, and nut clusters (a.k.a turtles) and newer treats. Tours and demonstrations of candy making are available (call to schedule group tours), and there is a candy museum onsite.

Scout Mountain Farm

VEGETABLES, FRUIT

2145 Scout Mountain Rd., Corydon IN 47112 (Harrison)
812-738-7196 • www.scoutmountainfarm.com

On this first-generation family farm, Margaret and Mike Schad grow apples, wine grapes, and a large variety of heirloom vegetables (tomatoes, eggplant, okra, herbs)—"plants that are special to your heart as well as to your palate." They sell them at their onsite farm market (call for opening hours) as well as at area farmers' markets. They plan to start making wine from their own grapes in 2008.

Wall Street Café

RESTAURANT

402 Wall St., Jeffersonville IN 47130 (Clark)
812-288-6466

Jerry Ramser and his wife, Mary, have been running the Wall Street Café for 25 years, and their specialty is ham—hand-sliced, house-cured, house-smoked country hams. The process is labor-intensive but they do it the old-fashioned way—it takes nearly 24 hours to prepare a country ham from scratch, starting with locally raised pork. The cooking, as you might guess, is down-home. Country ham with greens, corn bread, green beans, and sweet potatoes is a specialty, as are ham and eggs and the Great Wallburger—a half-pound hamburger. Arrive hungry!

Home Grown Indiana

250

WHY GRASS-FED BEEF?

"Grass-fed" is a popular buzz word in the food world these days, especially since Michael Pollan made graphically clear in The Omnivore's Dilemma what can be involved in "grain-finishing" cattle bound for the meat market. Just as the word "organic" carries the reassuring implication that our food is safe to eat, "grass-fed," when used to describe beef, implies that somewhere behind that juicy steak lived a happy cow, grazing in a field, unsullied by growth hormones or antibiotics.

And just like the word "organic," once "grass-fed" was seen to help sell product, everyone wanted a piece of it. Is a cow "grass-fed" if it is confined and fed grass harvested for it by a machine? Does "grass-fed" mean drug-free? As the federal government moves to define the term (with help from concerned lobbyists from the meat industry), some small farmers are switching to the term "pastured" to signify that their animals have been raised naturally and allowed to range freely.

Why the fuss? Fans of grass-fed beef claim that allowing cattle to eat only the grass that nature intended them to eat is not only good for the environment (not growing feed grain eliminates the need for chemical fertilizers and exhaust-spewing farm equipment) but also better for the cows, and thus better for the people who eat them.

Most farmers, however, confine their cattle and fatten them on corn before slaughtering them, a force-feeding that produces richly marbled meat but may result in sick, stressed animals that are routinely given antibiotics in their feed to keep them healthy. The meat we get is consequently not only loaded with chemicals (antibiotics, hormones to promote growth, and pesticides from the grain) but it is full of the kind of fat that makes us sick too—raising our cholesterol levels and clogging our arteries.

Devotees claim that meat from grass-fed cattle is healthier not only because it does not contain drugs or chemicals but because it has less saturated fat and more omega-3 fatty acids, essential fats that actually lower cholesterol and promote healthy hearts. Furthermore, they claim, the health benefits of grass-fed cows extend to their milk, and the cheese and butter made from it as well. (More information on these claims is available at www.westonaprice.org.)

They also say grass-fed beef tastes better—a little gamier and more beeflike, less fatty and soft. Because so many people find its taste superior, more and more restaurants are putting it on the menu, even though, because it is leaner, it requires careful cooking. Some are even having a hard time finding enough to satisfy the demand.

It is true (and confusing) that all young beef cattle are grass-fed, but not all of them are grass-finished. In Indiana, we are lucky to have a choice. Businesses like Apple Family Farm (p. 110), Traders Point (p. 132), Fiedler Farms (p. 239), and the Swiss Connection (p. 168) raise pastured, grass-finished animals, drug-free and often organic, whether they have been certified organic or not. Other farmers, like Dave Fischer of Fischer Farms, do confine their cattle and finish them on grain, but do it in humane conditions that allow them to raise the animals naturally, without hormones or drugs. How do you know what you are buying? One advantage of buying at local markets is that you can always ask.

EATING LOCAL WHILE DINING OUT

Bistro New Albany
148 E. Market St., New Albany IN 47150 (Floyd)
812-949-5227 • www.newalbanybistro.com

Blue River Café
128 Main St., Milltown IN 47145 (Crawford)
812-633-7510 • www.bluerivercafe.com
See p. 234

Federal Hill Café
310 Pearl St., New Albany IN 47150 (Floyd)
812-948-6646

Joe Huber Family Farm and Restaurant
2421 Scottsville Rd., Starlight IN 47106 (Clark)
812-923-5255 • www.joehubers.com
See p. 243

Treet's Bakery Café
133 E. Market St., New Albany IN 47150 (Floyd)
812-945-5440 • www.treetscafe.com

Wall Street Café
402 Wall St., Jeffersonville IN 47130 (Clark)
812-288-6466
See p. 250

FARMERS' MARKETS

Clark County Farmers' Market (Charleston)
On the Square
Charleston IN 47111 (Clark)
June–September, Thursdays 3:00 to 6:00 PM
www.jeffmainstreet.org/farmers_market

Clark County Farmers' Market (Jeffersonville)
Market Street between Spring and Pearl Streets
Jeffersonville IN 47131 (Clark)
Tuesdays 3:00 to 6:00 PM; June–September,
    Saturdays 9:30 AM to 12:30 PM
www.jeffmainstreet.org/farmers_market

Corydon Farmers' Market (Courthouse Square)
300 N. Capitol Ave., Corydon IN 47112 (Harrison)
June–September, Tuesdays 8:00 AM to 12 noon

Corydon Farmers' Market (Jay-C Food Store)
389 Old Capital Plaza N.W., Corydon IN 47112 (Harrison)
June–September, Wednesdays 4:30 to 6:30 PM

Corydon Farmers' Market (Tractor Supply Company)
1935 Old Highway 135 N.W., Corydon IN 47112 (Harrison)
June–September, Saturdays 8:00 AM to 12 noon

English Farmers' Market
914 E. Hwy. 64, English IN 47118 (Crawford)
June–October, Saturdays 9:00 AM to 1:00 PM

Evansville Farmers' Market
4th St. between Locust and Walnut Streets
Evansville IN 47708 (Vanderburgh)
July–September, Fridays 7:00 AM to 2:30 PM

Madison Farmers' Market
300 E. Main St., Madison IN 47250 (Jefferson)
May–November, Tuesdays, Thursdays, and
    Saturdays 6:30 AM to 1:00 PM

New Albany State Street Farmers' Market
1303 State St., New Albany IN 47150 (Floyd)
June–October, Tuesdays 4:30 to 7:00 PM,
    Saturdays 9:00 AM to 1:00 PM

Switzerland County Farmers' Market
212 W. Main St., Vevay IN 47043 (Switzerland)
June–November, Wednesdays and Saturdays 7:00 AM to 12 noon

254   **WINERIES**

Huber Winery
19816 Huber Rd., Starlight IN 47106 (Clark)
812-923-WINE • www.huberwinery.com
See p. 241

Kauffman Winery
9901 Lower Mt. Vernon Rd., Mount Vernon IN 47620 (Posey)
812-985-3769

Lanthier Winery
123 Mill St., Madison IN 47250 (Jefferson)
800-41-WINES (419-4637) • www.lanthierwinery.com

Madison Vineyards Estate Winery
1456 E. 400 N., Madison IN 47250 (Jefferson)
812-273-6500 • www.madisonvineyards.com

The Ridge Winery
298 Hwy. 156, Vevay IN 47043 (Switzerland)
812-427-3380 • www.theridgewinery.com

Thomas Family Winery
208 E. 2nd St., Madison IN 47250 (Jefferson)
812-273-3755 • www.thomasfamilywinery.us

Turtle Run Winery
940 St. Peters Church Rd. N.E., Corydon IN 47112 (Harrison)
812-952-2650 • www.turtlerunwinery.com

Winzerwald Winery
26300 N. Indian Lake Rd., Bristow IN 47515 (Perry)
812-357-7000 • www.winzerwaldwinery.com

MICROBREWERIES & BREWPUBS

Little Cheers Restaurant and Pub
329 Main St., Evansville IN 47708 (Vanderburgh)
812-423-9740 • www.littlecheers.com

New Albanian Brewing Company
3312 Plaza Dr., New Albany IN 47150 (Floyd)
812-949-2804 • www.newalbanian.com

Turoni's Pizzery and Brewery
408 N. Main St., Evansville IN 47711 (Vanderburgh)
812-44-9873

Turoni's Forget-Me-Not Inn on the Eastside
4 N. Weinbach Ave., Evansville IN 47711 (Vanderburgh)
812-477-7500 • www.turonis.com

FOOD FESTIVALS

Indiana "Hot Luck" and Fiery Foods Exhibition
Madison IN (Jefferson)
Spicy foods
Early April
800-948-8466 • www.thomasfamilywinery.us

Madison Ribberfest
BBQ cook-off and lots more
Madison IN (Jefferson)
Mid-August
800-559-2956 • www.madisonribberfest.com

Mt. Zion Apple Harvest Festival
Famous apple dishes served and sold
Chrisney IN (Spencer)
1st of October
812-649-2753

Rising Sun Navy Bean Festival
Navy bean soup and fun for all
Rising Sun IN (Ohio)
Mid-October
812-438-3130 • www.enjoyrisingsun.com

St. John's Starlight Strawberry Festival
Strawberry shortcake
Starlight IN (Clark)
Late May
812-923-5785

Schocalade Celebration
Madison IN (Jefferson)
Chocolate and wine
2nd week of February
812-273-2409 • www.lanthierwinery.com

Swiss Wine Festival
Wine tasting, grape stomp, and lots of food
Vevay IN (Switzerland)
End of August
800-435-5688

Home Grown Indiana

LIST OF RECIPES

COUNTY INDEX

PRODUCT/TYPE INDEX

Christine Barbour teaches American politics and the politics of food at Indiana University Bloomington. She is also the food editor of *Bloom Magazine,* a freelance food writer and photographer whose work has appeared in, among other publications, *Indianapolis Monthly* and *Indianapolis dine,* and an avid food blogger at www .myplateoryours.net. She is the author (with Scott Feickert) of *Indiana Cooks! Great Restaurant Recipes for the Home Kitchen* and of two political science textbooks, and is currently working on a book about the fishing industry in Apalachicola, Florida. She is a founding member and co-director of Slow Food Bloomington.

Scott Hutcheson works in community and economic development for Purdue University. He also writes for *Indianapolis Monthly* and is the author of an award-winning syndicated newspaper column, The Hungry Hoosier. He writes and produces for *Across Indiana* on WFYI Indianapolis public television, contributes to the nationally distributed East Feed Midwest podcast, has a weekly radio show on WIRE, and is creator of the HungryHoosier .com website.